UNUSUALLY
STUPID
CELEBRITIES

UNUSUALLY STUPID CELEBRITIES

A COMPENDIUM OF ALL-STAR STUPIDITY

KATHRYN PETRAS
and ROSS PETRAS

VILLARD NEW YORK

A Villard Books Trade Paperback Original

Copyright © 2007 by Kathryn Petras and Ross Petras

Published in the United States by Villard Books, an imprint of
The Random House Publishing Group, a division of
Random House, Inc., New York.

VILLARD and "V" CIRCLED Design are registered trademarks of
Random House, Inc.

ISBN 978-0-8129-7750-9

Library of Congress Cataloging-in-Publication Data

Petras, Kathryn.
Unusually stupid celebrities: a compendium of all-star stupidity /
Kathryn Petras and Ross Petras.
p.   cm.
ISBN-13: 978-0-8129-7750-9 (pbk.)
ISBN-10: 0-8129-7750-5 (pbk.)
1. Celebrities—Anecdotes. 2. Stupidity—Anecdotes. 3. Stupidity—
Humor. I. Petras, Ross. II. Title.
CT105.P48 2007
081—dc22   2006100426

Printed in the United States of America

www.villard.com

2 4 6 8 9 7 5 3 1

Book design by Susan Turner

CONTENTS

INTRODUCTION

The average ancient Greek worshipped Zeus and Hera. The average ancient Roman worshipped Jupiter and Juno. The average modern human today worships [fill in any male and female celebrity here].

You can see how far we've come in the past two thousand years.

But at least we modern humans aren't sacrificing goats to, say, Christina Aguilera. (As far as we know. . . . Although there *is* this guy next door and last night we heard a strange bleating sound. Oh, never mind.)

Back to our point: Celebrities are popular. That's pretty much what makes them celebrities.

So—in the spirit of all our other "stupid" works, we decided it was time to examine this peculiar (literally) and fascinating subset: to wit, unusually stupid *celebrities.* We chose to focus on celebrities for several reasons: a) they do a lot of stupid things; b) a lot is written about them; c) people like to read about them; and d) they make a lot more money than we do and we'd like to get our little cut.

Unusually Stupid Celebrities covers a cross section of

stupid (and annoying) celebrity behavior divided into fourteen chapters. All the information is true, to the best of our knowledge. And names have not been changed to protect the guilty.

As for the innocent? There aren't too many in here.

UNUSUALLY STUPID CELEBRITIES

THE CONCERNED CELEBRITY
Celebrities on the World Around Us

CELEBRITIES ARE LIKE SUPERHEROES—they are powerful beings who can use their special skills for good. Or evil, for that matter.

So let us take a look at how celebrities use their power on the world stage.

Celebrities Solve All the World's Problems, Part 1

It is terribly easy—and terribly unfair—to dismiss celebrities as mere pretty faces. These people are *thinkers* and *carers* and *doers.* Like so many of us, they worry about the world of today, about the pressing problems we face. And, as so-called "creatives," they are chock-full of extremely creative (not to mention innovative) suggestions on how to solve these problems. We are shocked, *shocked,* that no one has ever acted upon these ideas.

Let us take a look, then, at some of the most pressing problems existing in the 21st century—and the solutions proposed by various celebrities.

World Problem #1: Terrorism

Celebrity Solution: Put "all the mean people" in a special terrorist country

Tara Reid is one helluva prognosticator. In fact, we wonder why she has never been a talking head on CNN. (Open note to CNN: Sign this gal up!) After the London terrorist subway bombings, she came up with a sage idea on how to prevent further terrorism:

> "I wish all the mean people, if you want to be mean to each other, just buy a country together and blow each other up. Then we'd have no terrorists left. Like, don't kill innocent people for no reason. It's not fair. We love everybody. We'd even like them if they said they're sorry. It's not fair that innocent people are getting hurt. It makes me sad."

And this makes us sad too.

World Problem #2: The high crime rate

Celebrity Solution: Nudity on television

Why listen to endless debates about the pros and cons of gun control? The issue, apparently, isn't about bearing arms, but *baring* arms . . . and breasts . . . and everything else. Or, to put it more succinctly—as rapper and erstwhile social reformer Nelly sums it up:

> "I could turn on just about any television channel in Europe and see full nudity. And their crime rate is a lot lower than ours. Go figure."

Excellent point, Nelly!

World Problem #3: The environment
Celebrity Solution: Educate yourself

Yes, this sounds a little simplistic, but as any celebrity could tell you, it's *vital* to keep up with studies about pollution, the greenhouse effect, global warming, etc. It's not enough to just drive a Prius. Instead, we should all take a page from actress Kate Bosworth's book and be students of environmental issues. Know the facts! Learn everything you can! This will enable you to make the right choices to protect Mother Earth. Just listen to her commentary:

> "There was just a study done actually, I saw it on Regis and Kelly, I can't remember how many hours a year a person uses being in their car in L.A., but it's, like, a lot of time."

World Problem #3a: The environment
Another Celebrity Solution: Shit in the woods

Drew Barrymore realizes the way to saving the environment is for all of us to live more in tune with nature. Drew—who, incidentally, earns about $15 million a film—spent some time in a primitive Chilean village for an MTV series. "I aspire to be like them more," she raved (perhaps ignoring their high infant mortality rate and short life expectancies). Highlight of her visit?

> "I took a poo in the woods hunched over like an animal. It was awesome."

World Problem #4: War
Celebrity Solution: Anus-smelling

Actor Dustin Hoffman puts his proboscis in the, er, meat of the matter when it comes to preventing war:

"When a lot of dogs are on the beach, the first thing they do is smell each other's asses. The information that's gotten somehow makes pacifists out of all of them. I've thought, 'If only we smelled each other's asses, there wouldn't be any war.' "

(Note: Hoffman, unfortunately, did not offer further explanations on how to decipher the meaning of said ass-scents, nor did he delineate the preferred method of ass-smelling.)

World Problem #5: Nuclear waste disposal
Celebrity Solution: Kabbalah water

Okay, yes, it *was* Madonna who came up with this solution. (How did you guess?)

Concerned about the possibility of an ecological disaster due to too much nuclear waste, she and hubby Guy "Yes, I Am a Director, Not Just Her Husband" Ritchie began lobbying the British government and nuclear industry to let them know they had the perfect answer: Kabbalah water, a "mystical" liquid that helps do pretty much anything and everything—including, clearly, defanging nuclear waste. And they had proof!—well, "claims"—that the magic fluid already has worked on Russian nuclear waste.

Sadly, scientists and government officials aren't as prescient as Madge and remain naysayers. Said one, "It was like a crank call . . . the scientific mechanisms and principles were just bollocks, basically."

World Problem #6: Too much negativity
Celebrity Solution: Positivity!

One final problem and solution—and this one is of a more general nature. We are speaking of the relentless negativity that pervades this world. How can we rid our planet of this negative energy? How can we turn from the dark to the light? Kate Bosworth knows, and it's really all just so simple, we're shocked no one has thought of it before:

> "If you, like, have everybody taking ten minutes a day and really focusing on, like, positivity and a better world and a better self, like, imagine all that, just all that positivity going out there."

> Oh, yeah, baby! We can dig it!

Celebrities' Great Contributions to Humanity

Some stars go one step further. They not only suggest, they *contribute* to humankind. They sacrifice themselves to the higher good, they walk the lonely walk. For themselves? No—for their fans, for their fellow countrymen (and women). In short, for us *all*.

Celebrity Humanitarian: Rapper Diddy (Sean Combs)
Great Contribution to Humanity: Getting rid of the "P" from his name

It was tough, perhaps, but he had to do it, explained Diddy, once known as P. Diddy. His relationship with his fans was important and yet he felt himself somehow becoming separated from them. What to do? He decided to sacrifice of an integral part of *himself.* . . .

> "I felt like the 'P' was coming between me and my fans. We had to simplify it. It was, you know, during concerts and half the crowd saying 'P. Diddy' and

half the crowd chanting 'Diddy.' Now everybody can just chant 'Diddy.' "

The man may have lost his initial "P," but grateful fans will cherish the sacrifice. For now they *all* can chant, "Diddy."

Celebrity Humanitarian: Supermodel Fabio
Great Contribution to Humanity: Speaking out publicly on the dangers of getting hit in the head by flying birds that live near roller coasters at theme parks

Sometimes it needs someone famous to alert the public to lurking hidden dangers. In superbuff Fabio's case his mission began with a seemingly innocent promotional ride on Busch Gardens Williamsburg's new Apollo's Chariot roller coaster. Unfortunately, during the promotional roller coaster ride, Fabio's face suffered a mid-ride collision with a flying bird (reportedly a goose) that ended in a bloody human-avian mess.

The supermodel, blood streaming from his nose, was taken to a nearby hospital, treated for a minor cut, and released. The goose, alas, did not fare as well; someone reported a dead goose floating in a nearby body of water.

In eloquent but broken English, the charming hardheaded Italian hunk related the very real dangers of being-hit-in-the-head-by-flying-birds-while-riding-on-a-rollercoaster on the TV morning shows, and issued a gentle but firm statement urging Busch Gardens "now" to install safety measures so "that this will not happen again." He also warned the world of the important dangers of building theme parks with roller coaster rides near avian nesting or breeding areas.

The model, whose favorite color is turquoise and who

adorns romance novel covers and serves as a spokesperson for I Can't Believe It's Not Butter, sternly added that a similar incident "could cause more serious accidents or possibly a child's death."

Unfortunately, as one paper reported, "nationwide accident data involving birds, roller-coaster riders and birds versus roller-coaster riders were not immediately available."

Celebrity Humanitarian: Soccer star David Beckham
Great Contribution to Humanity: Shaves mohawk haircut—for the children

Another child-oriented celebrity, superstar soccer player David Beckham, quite charitably chose to abandon his famous Mohawk haircut. He was very concerned about children copying his hairstyle and getting into trouble.

Instead, the L.A. Galaxy player, then with Manchester United, decided to adopt a new, more mature style: He shaved off half of his eyebrow.

Later he shaved three lines in his eyebrow in a tribute to his megabucks-paying sponsor, triple-striped Adidas, actions which children presumably can comfortably emulate, their parents certainly understanding the value of lucrative sponsorships.

Celebrity Humanitarian: Actor David Hasselhoff
Great Contribution to Humanity: In a word, *Baywatch*

According to "the Hoff," his TV show about buff and buffette lifeguards in L.A. was more than just a show about tits, ass, pecs, and abs. It was *significant:*

"Beyond its entertainment value, *Baywatch* has enriched and, in many cases, helped save lives."

Two modest questions, Herr Hoff-meister: How did it enrich? Whom did it save?

Celebrity Humanitarian: Actress Demi Moore

Great Contribution to Humanity: Faces down cost-cutting selfish accountant types and travels with makeup artist, hairstylist, personal assistant, chef, and three nannies—for the "higher good"

Demi Moore, no stranger to charity and caring for others, traveled with such a large entourage in 1997 that she used two private jets. She explained that the immense expense of flying this entourage was justifiable. "We're working together for the higher good." The higher good in question was promoting her not-so-classic film *GI Jane.*

(Later, while promoting the film *Ghost,* Moore included a masseuse, fashion consultant, an assistant and an assistant's assistant in her traveling retinue—but as *Ghost* did better at the box office, we may safely assume this was a higher "Higher Good.")

Celebrity Humanitarian: Model Naomi Campbell

Great Contribution to Humanity: Modeling

Martin Luther King, Jr., may have stirred millions with his courageous eloquence, but Naomi Campbell is making her own contribution to civil rights for African Americans.

The high-priced supermodel, who takes home at least several million a year and was recently estimated to be worth about $30 million, models for fashion magazines not for herself, but for others. (Naturally she keeps the money and the perks—it is the modeling *itself* which is her contribution.)

As she explains, "I look at [modeling] as something I'm doing for black people in general."

We're certain many are pleased with such *selfless* generosity.

Celebrity Humanitarian: Singer Michael Jackson
Great Contribution to Humanity: Participation in halftime show at Super Bowl

In the singer's own words, "I can't think of a better way to spread the message of world peace than by working with the NFL and being part of Super Bowl XXVII."

Actually, we kind of think we could think of a lot of better ways, but maybe we're just being cynical.

Celebrities Contribute to Racism (and Anti-Semitism Too!)

Some celebrities go the extra mile and speak their special truths—unafraid of public reaction. True, some of their opinions may be a little . . . out there.

You might think that with the mikes on and the cameras rolling, your average celebrity would watch his or her mouth in our politically correct world. But sometimes, as with Mel Gibson's famous DUI episode, a little alcohol loosens the ol' tongue.

And then there are *other* celebrities, too, bolder ones than old Mel, ones who don't even need alcohol and traffic cops to opine rather vigorously—some would say maybe a mite intolerantly—on the different races and people that make up our marvelously diverse world.

Here, then, a somewhat *gloves-off* celebrity take on some minorities.

Jews Caused All the Wars in the World

Vietnam? The Jews. The Battle of Hastings? The Jews. The Civil War? Yup, the Jews. Okay, if you hadn't heard it yet, for some reason, now you know. Or you're reminded again. Courtesy of actor Mel Gibson:

> "Fucking Jews . . . the Jews are responsible for all the wars in the world."

After sharing these stunningly advanced and deep geopolitical insights, Gibson asked a deputy who had stopped him for drunk driving: "Are you a Jew?"

Good question in this case, just maybe. (Incidentally, the deputy *was* Jewish.)

Arabs Should Be Nuked and Their Cities Turned into Molten Green Glass Parking Lots

On the other side of the proverbial coin from Mel Gibson is genius actor James "Kill Those Ragheads" Woods, who boasts an IQ of 180 and SAT scores of 779 and 800 (see page 18). Did we mention that Woods has an IQ of over 180 and SAT scores of 779 and 800? Or has Woods already told you?

Anyway, James Woods is against negotiating with "any of these crappy little Arab states" and says that if he had any evidence at all that any single country was supporting "even a single ounce" of terrorism, "I would say wipe them off the face of the earth." He adds approvingly that had terrorism happened to the Russians, "about three major cities in the Middle East would have been parking lots in twenty minutes. They would have been molten green glass, not a single thing would have lived there for 250,000 years. . . ." (One question to our actor with the large brainpan: How do you park in molten green glass?)

Woods, with his IQ of 180, apparently doesn't think that the millions of *innocent* Arabs in these cities which harbor few terrorists have any right to live, which seems a bit uncaring to us. Moreover, it does not seem to be a particularly *intelligent* approach to terrorism. But then again, Woods only got 779 on the math portion of his SATs, not a perfect 800.

Indians Are Short, Poor, Dark, and Don't Speak English

This fascinating and perhaps controversial insight comes from a rather obscure celebrity (but we bet she's big on the pampas)—none other than the 2004 Miss Bolivia herself, Gabriela Oviedo. She offered these observations in Ecuador, where the Miss Universe pageant was being held:

"Unfortunately, people that don't know Bolivia very much think that we are all just Indian people . . . poor people and very short people and Indian people. I'm from the other side of the country . . . and we are tall and we are white people and we know English."

No, we must admit we were unaware of this. But we now can see the *educational* value of the Miss Universe pageant. Look what we just learned about Bolivia!

Negroes Look Like Cannibals

Singer Nico offered up this somewhat illogical perception of African Americans, but at least she did acknowledge it was a mistake. Not the sentiments themselves, of course, but saying them. That is, people took it so *harshly,* when all she said was . . .

"I made a mistake. I said in *Melody Maker* to some interviewer that I didn't like Negroes. That's all.

They took it so personally . . . although it's a whole different race. I mean, Bob Marley doesn't resemble a Negro, does he? . . . He's an archetype of Jamaican . . . but with the features like white people. I don't like the features. They're so much like animals . . . it's cannibals, no?"

We're surprised too that people took this so personally. What's *wrong* with people?

Blacks, Women, and Jews Are Not That Great

At least, not according to comedian Michael Richards, an equal-opportunity "let's spread the hate" kinda guy. There's more than enough to go around!

We all know about the famous rant he unleashed upon two black hecklers at the Comedy Store:

> "Fifty years ago we'd have you upside down with a fucking fork up your ass! You can talk, you can talk, you can talk! You're brave now, motherfucker. Throw his ass out, he's a nigger. He's a nigger! He's a nigger! A nigger! Look, there's a nigger!"

Ah, yes. We're, um, sure it was taken out of context. . . .
But then the public learned about some earlier outbursts. To a female comedian, another riff, this time with "cunt" substituted for "nigger":

> "You will never work in this town again. . . . I'll make sure of that, you little cunt. . . . You're a cunt . . . dirty little cunt."

And to Jewish hecklers, the very plain and simple:

> "You're a fucking Jew. Your people are the cause of Jesus dying."

The final word on this debacle from *Star* magazine editor at large Jill Dobson: It was "a very bad PR move."

Celebrities Solve All the World's Problems, Part 2
(Unsung Celebrity Heroes—or, Move Over, Mother Teresa)

Forget dancing, singing, acting. Some celebrities do far more—or, actually, *are* far more. They're unsung geniuses, fantastic humanitarians, great scientists.

Sadly, we non-celebrities too often don't give credit where credit is due. Did you know, for example, David Hasselhoff's role in bringing democracy to Europe?

If not, read on and learn.

DAVID HASSELHOFF: Responsible for Tearing Down the Berlin Wall and Ending Communism

Who would have thought that this aging beach stud, star of *Baywatch* (that inspiring T&A show about buff lifeguards on an L.A. beach), would actually be the one human responsible for tearing down the Berlin Wall, that evil stone symbol of the Cold War that separated free West Berlin from Communist East Berlin?

Well, the Hoff was the *one*.

Sadly, the world doesn't know. Hasselhoff himself complained to the curators of the Berlin Museum at Checkpoint Charlie that there was a significant omission on the walls of the museum—namely a photograph of himself and recognition of his great political role in reunifying the two Germanies.

How did "The Great Buff 'n' Tan Reunifier of Germany" do it? How did he pretty much single-handedly end Communist oppression in Eastern Europe?

By singing one of his songs, of course. In 1989 a younger and even more buff Hoff went to West Berlin's Brandenburg Gate and sang "Looking for Freedom" (*freedom*, get it?) to millions of German fans. He "personally moved the people"—to such a degree that they simply and spontaneously began tearing down the wall! "After my appearance," Hasselhoff recalled, "I hacked away at pieces of the wall that had the black, red and yellow colors of the German flag on it. I kept the big piece for myself and gave the smaller pieces to colleagues at *Baywatch*." Anticommunist—and a caring, giving guy.

Hasselhoff admitted that many of his German fans didn't speak English and maybe didn't even understand the song, but he still insists he was responsible. Way to go, Hoffman!

TOM CRUISE: Gets Heroin Addicts off Heroin in Only Three Days

Forget methadone. Forget costly psychiatrists, lengthy "cold turkey" hospital stays, forget the billions that have been spent researching the problems of addiction and depression. *Tom Cruise has the answers. He can get addicts off in a few days. He can cure depression.*

A Scientologist and a high school dropout, Cruise is a profound student of psychiatry. Like all great pioneers, particularly those without any medical qualifications at all, he sometimes is misunderstood. As part of his selfless campaigning for his psychiatric views, Cruise often has to get tough, as in this exchange with talk show host Matt Lauer. Lauer actually said that sometimes antidepressants were good for you, and said he personally knew people who had been helped. And so Cruise admonished the ignorant Lauer.

CRUISE: ". . . to talk about it in a way of saying, 'Well, isn't it okay?' and being reasonable about it when you don't know and I do, I think that you should be a little bit more responsible in knowing what it is."

LAUER: "But—"

CRUISE: "Because you—you communicate to people."

LAUER: "But you're now telling me that your experiences with the people I know, which are zero, are more important than my experiences."

CRUISE: "What do you mean by that?"

LAUER: "You're telling me what's worked for people I know hasn't worked for people I know. I'm telling you I've lived with these people and they're better."

CRUISE: "So, you're—you're advocating it?"

Unfettered by Lauer's impeccable logic, Cruise ignored the irritating details and brilliantly clinched the argument: "Here's the problem. You don't know the history of psychiatry. I do."

Indeed the thriller actor does, if he says so himself. (And he does say so. Frequently.)

So why are pills so bad for psychiatric problems? All they do "is mask the problem. . . . And if you understand the history of it, it masks the problem. That's what it does. That's all it does. There is no such thing as a chemical imbalance."

Most modern psychiatrists would disagree, but who are they compared to Tom Cruise? Did any one of them make $62 million in one year? They've only studied chemistry, not only in high school but in college and med school.

And what about those heroin addicts? Using Tom's and Scientology's advanced detox techniques, he says he can get someone off heroin fairly quickly. He's done it. "I think it's appalling that people have to live a life of drug addiction when I have personally helped people get off drugs."

Tom Cruise. Actor, Scientist, Humanist.

JAMES WOODS: An Einsteinian Genius Who Has an IQ of 180 and Got 779 and 800 on His SATs

Some people are great simply by *being*.

Such a person is James Woods.

The genius actor has an IQ of over 180 and got a 779 and 800 on the math and English parts of his SATs. We mention it here again even though it is hard living on Planet Earth and escaping these facts: James Woods somehow seems to have had it mentioned *everywhere*—proof of his great mind, at least in the PR area.

Googling the phrase "James Woods" on a random day in February 2007 got us 1,280,000 citations, and most of the ones we read stated that James Woods has an IQ of 180 and received 779 on the math and 800 on the English portions of his SATs. Try it yourself sometime. Some of these websites mention that the IQ test was the Stanford-Binet IQ test, in case you're interested. As virtually every other star does not publicize his or her IQ or SAT scores, we feel that James Woods should be applauded for being a genius, since he obviously feels that it is an essential part of his being. In his words, "I'm so extremely intelligent that it's actually harmed my career as an actor."

After somehow having it brought up virtually everywhere, Woods complains about it, too.

"Yeah, I scored 800 on the verbal part of the SATs and

CELEBRITY CONTRIBUTIONS TO TORTURE

It's heartening to know that your songs are appreciated, but it's another thing to learn that they're used as WCDs—weapons of celebrity destruction—to torture and intimidate fellow human beings. But some singers are more dangerous than half a pound of weapons-grade plutonium.

....

Barry Manilow's Love Songs Are Australia's Secret Weapon Against Juvenile Delinquents

Officials in Rockdale, Australia, are broadcasting Barry Manilow's greatest hits over loudspeakers to discourage drag racers. Not surprisingly, it is working.

Manilow, however, is not amused. And he doesn't think it's working because the drag racers hate what some would call saccharine music. "If you played *anyone's* music for that long, you'd drive any rationally minded human out of their mind [our italics]. But have they thought that these hoodlums might like my music? What if some of them began to sing along with 'Can't Smile Without You'? . . . What if this actually attracts more hoodlums—puts smiles on their faces?" Deputy Mayor Bill Saravinovski is not convinced. In his words: "Barry's our secret weapon."

....

Guantánamo Bay Interrogators Torture 9/11 Hijacking Suspects by Playing Christina Aguilera Music

When Mohammed al-Qahtani, the purported "20th hijacker" and a compatriot of Osama bin Laden, wouldn't talk, U.S. interrogators knew what to do. According to *Time* magazine, while he dozed off, interrogators roused him by "dripping water on his head or playing Christina Aguilera music."

And yet the U.S. government still has the *audacity* to claim that it does not use torture at Guantánamo.

....

CIA Safe House Interrogators Prefer Red Hot Chili Peppers for Optimal Torture

CIA interrogators at secret safe houses in Thailand reportedly utilized the rock music of the Red Hot Chili Peppers to soften up captured terrorists. We do not know why they prefer this to Xtina.

....

U.S. Army Uses AC/DC, Billy Idol, and Bruce Cockburn Songs to Fight Enemies and Terrorists

The Army, no stranger to the *power* of music, has used AC/DC at the siege of Fallujah in Iraq; and Billy Idol and Bruck Cockburn at the siege of Panamanian dictator Manuel Noriega during Operation Just Cause in 1989.

We're not sure when and if the CD of Army Weaponized Rock Songs will be released.

779 on the math. Why does everybody talk about this? Who gives a shit?"

But then he *brings it up again.*

"I was a straight A student in high school and I never did anything but show up. . . . I took the Stanford-Binet IQ test, and I guess 180 is the highest it will go, and I got them all right. I didn't miss one. My score was 180 plus."

THE CONCERNED CELEBRITY ★ 21

The Giving Celebrity: The Give and, Particularly, the Take of Celebrity Charitable Contributions

As with great humanitarians like Mother Teresa, Gandhi, and Martin Luther King, Jr., celebrities like to help. They want to give a little of themselves to all those Little People out there—the poor, the average, the hardworking students, soldiers defending our freedoms, charitable organizations doing good deeds.

Of course, *unlike* those great humanitarians like Mother Teresa, Gandhi, and Martin Luther King, Jr., celebrities have certain minor needs, or should we say *requests*. . . .

Pop Star Geri Halliwell

Charitable Contribution: Entertaining the soldiers in Iraq who daily face gunfire and bombs

Minor Requests: Air-conditioned tents with a working refrigerator, stocked with soy milk and fruit juices. Also irons, ironing boards, clothing racks, and, of course, a desert computer with full Internet access.

Psych Star Dr. Laura Schlesinger

Charitable Contribution: Imparting her psychological wisdom before the Jewish Welfare Federation

Minor Requests: First, a five-star hotel room without a "funny smell." Similarly, transportation without such smells.

Dr. Laura turned down the best suite at the Grand Kempinski Dallas Hotel, and following that, three others. She finally agreed that the Mansion on Turtle Creek was suitable; but she had some issues with the food offered there. She was picked up for the speech by a private car, but found that the car, too, "smelled." Someone had worn perfume. So she got out and hailed a cab. Unfortunately, the cab also "smelled," and so did another. And another. Finally finding a cab that didn't smell, the good doctor arrived and made her speech. Afterward, although she had received a $30,000 honorarium to mingle with guests, Dr. Laura was not friendly at the donor reception and left quickly, also leaving behind gifts from her hosts. But this wasn't all. According to one member of the audience: "The worst was how unpleasant and irritating she was in her speech. Before the evening was over, she had offended almost every woman in the room. There was barely any applause. Some people walked out. I felt like it."

After catching flak when a newspaper article appeared about this, an embarrassed Dr. Laura suddenly decided she would donate her hard-earned dough to a home for unwed mothers.

Radio News Personality Sean Hannity

Charitable Contribution: "Volunteered" to speak at Utah Valley State College, and Washington University in St. Louis

Minor Request: Reimbursement for travel expenses

A humble and innocuous request, perhaps, but Hannity takes the "expense" part of travel very literally: In the case of his speech at the nonprofit Utah Valley State College, he asked for a cool $49,850. Later Hannity accepted another speaking engagement at Washington University in St. Louis. Perhaps fearful of the radio personality's penchant for ultra-fat expense accounts, the university offered him first-class airplane tickets, which he refused; then it offered him use of a private jet, which he also refused; in fact, he then proceeded to cancel the speaking engagement. But at least upright Hannity seemed contrite. Perhaps well aware of the uncharitable nature of Hannity's action, a representative reportedly asked students not to disclose the reasons for the cancellation.

Actress Mischa Barton

Charitable Contribution: Two very minor efforts: walking down the runway for "Race to Erase MS" event, and attending a benefit for helptheterrorvictims.org

Minor Request: Designer dresses

Barton's attitude seemed to basically be: How much do I get? In her own words: "Tommy Hilfiger picked that dress for me, and it felt very cool and flappery. But I was like, 'There's no way I'm walking down the runway. You couldn't pay me enough money.' And they were like, 'C'mon, it's charity. Please. Tommy will give you the best dress.' I was so happy when it was over."

Barton's take on a Russian terror victims' benefit shows the same Mother Teresa–like selflessness: "[It was] for these Russian victims of, like, acts of terror. Most of the people had no idea who I was because they were all into this thing about helping Russian children. But I was so glad I went. That's [where I got] my favorite jacket ever. It's so horribly '80s, but it's vintage YSL. It cost me nothing."

TV Therapist Dr. Phil McGraw

Charitable Contribution: Keynote speaker at a charity obesity forum hosted by the first lady of California, Maria Shriver

Minor Requests: Introduction by a Very Important Person (Arnold Schwarzenegger) as befits a Very Important TV Therapist. Plus personal bathroom.

When Dr. Phil arrived at the forum, he learned that Arnold would be unable to do his intro—at which point the good doctor did what any good therapist would tell his patients to do: he threw a tantrum. "No one told me," he claimed. "But we called you several times," staffers explained. "No, you didn't!" he pouted. "I'm not happy," he said, and petulantly added that he wasn't going to do the show after all. Maria Shriver, perhaps a little tired of the "communication skills" he was exhibiting, suggested he leave. Then the shit hit the fan—almost literally—when the good doctor asked to use the bathroom first and learned it was a *public* bathroom. Needless to say, Dr. Phil was absolutely horrified, explaining that he never used public facilities. Maria said, "Well, that's the only one we have. Use it or not. Take your camera crew and go." After the doctor went to the bathroom, he announced, "I might as well stay now that I'm here." Maria remained unimpressed with his attempts at reconciliation, explaining that he didn't have to. "My seven-year-old doesn't act the way you do."

Singer Jennifer Lopez

Charitable Contribution: Performing at New York's Olympic torch ceremony

Minor Requests: Private round-trip jet to and from Miami, at a cost of over $38,600; a $9,500 a night hotel suite, two $1,000 bedrooms for her bodyguard and assistant, $4,500 for hairstyling, $6,000 for makeup

According to the New York *Daily News,* the city government couldn't justify spending all that much taxpayer money on the rapacious diva, and Lopez canceled the engagement, citing "work commitments." Later her PR spokesperson defended Lopez, saying that "she was assured it wasn't the taxpayers' money and it was actually private donors."

2

THE CELEBRITY BODY

LET'S TAKE A BREATHER from the problems of the world and move on to something more important. Something that occupies much more of the American mind than problems of the environment, world affairs, or the economy.

We're talking celebrity bods.

Problem Breasts: When Celebrity Breasts Go Bad

Let's get something off our chests. (Sorry. It was unavoidable. We won't do it again.) We know breasts can be fun. People like them. They're generally a good thing. But there is a little-discussed darker side to celebrity breasts. (No, not underneath Pamela Anderson's globes. We're speaking more generally here.)

We feel compelled to warn you that breasts can be beastly. "Fun bags" are sometimes not so fun. Melons can induce melancholia. And so on. Consider these cautionary tales about the havoc a breast (or two) can wreak.

Pamela Anderson's Breast Causes Commotion in Restaurant

Pamela Anderson was enjoying a nice dinner at da Maurizio restaurant in Halifax, Nova Scotia, when all hell broke loose—or, more correctly, leaked out.

Fellow diners noticed Anderson start shrieking, clutching her right breast, and screaming "Something popped!" One eyewitness described the scene: "At first I thought she was having a heart attack. But then something started to ooze right into her soup. I'm not sure what it was, but it was pretty gross."

Indeed. But the sight didn't deter an attentive restaurant staffer, who rushed to the rescue—helpfully proffering a large water glass. Pam's dining companion, former race car driver Eddie Irvine, shoved said glass under her breast in a futile effort to prop it up and, presumably, to catch any leakage. The pair shuffled out—with Irvine holding the glass under Pam's golden globe while Pam kept telling him to forget about it.

Following this event, Anderson canceled her appearance as host of the Canadian Music Awards. Her spokesperson explained this was due to "a medical emergency." The restaurant had no comment on the incident other than to say that "the restaurant is equipped for most, if not all, forms of emergency."

Courtney Love's Breast Kills Dog

Back in 2002 when Courtney Love was on her self-improvement kick, she decided to get her implants removed to go to a more natural and less inflated look. (Apparently, she decided to have her lips inflated instead, but that's neither here nor there.) But, having lived with the gooshy pouches for so long, Love decided to take them home as souvenirs.

Sadly, her dog mistook the old fun bags for new fun toys—and died after choking on one of them.

Lindsay Lohan's Breasts May Have Potential to Offend Family Audiences

Lindsay Lohan—she who has gone from busty to flat to super-busty (and says it's all due to fluctuating weight, something we all believe)—had a work-related breast problem. Or, more specifically, Disney did.

Back before Lohan got very thin and quite flat, then a little fuller figured and *incredibly* large-chested, she was blessed with a rather voluptuous bustline for a teenybopper starlet. Which was a bit of a problem when she starred in the Disney film *Herbie: Fully Loaded*. (Note: The term "fully loaded" does not refer to Lohan.)

Several sources reported that after test screenings of the film, parents objected to Lohan's character—or rather, certain *attributes* of her character. To wit, her breasts. Said breasts bounced a bit too much when she jumped up and down at a racetrack. Disney execs got worried that Lindsay's lady lumps could kill the chances of the film's G-rating. So Disney technicians reportedly had to give Lohan a digital breast reduction (she lost two cup sizes) and a digital fashion makeover (plunging necklines were raised).

The film's director, Angela Robinson, however, denied the story. Flatly.

Tara Reid's Breast Escapes . . . Then Spawns Lawsuit

Tara Reid's breast is a frisky little (we use the word "little" euphemistically, not literally) critter. It is a paparazzo's best friend and seems to love the limelight.

Its first major public outing was at P. Diddy's birthday

party at Cipriani Downtown in New York. While Tara posed for photographers, her dress fell . . . and her larger-than-in-the-past breast was caught on film—for quite some time, at that.

At the time, Tara found the incident, the resulting pictures, and the inevitable hubbub amusing, even piquant. "You would think people had never seen a boob before. I've never seen anything like it! You would think my boob had popped out and shot Gandhi! From the way people reacted I thought I'd got it out and choked someone to death with it."

And that was that—until a full-page ad in *Vegas* magazine for Sky Las Vegas Condominiums referred to the boob slippage—with the classy headline: "Dear Tara Reid, come let it all hang out."

Tara slapped the company with a lawsuit, suing for unspecified damages for "humiliation, embarrassment and mental anguish," claiming they used her name without permission and "defamed" and "ridiculed" her by implying she was "sexually lewd and/or immoral."

(Note: Even though after the Diddy slip, Tara said, "My hooters are under control! I'm taped up now, totally. I'm using double tape. Double double tape. My boobs are going nowhere ever again," her breast *has* popped out a few more times. We have no word on any other pending ads and/or lawsuits connected to these recent breast escapes.)

Kate Beckinsale's Breasts Reportedly Require Special Contract Clause

Some breasts are contractually challenging. Like Kate Beckinsale's—whose breasts reportedly warrant a clause saying she can't be filmed bending over at more than a 45-degree angle.

Why 45 degrees? "Because her boob implants slide up to her collar bone."

This is the claim of fellow British thespian Sienna Guillory—star of such important films as *Resident Evil 2*—who wanted to let the press know that Kate has changed since she went Hollywood.

Beckinsale's agent categorically denies the charges, explaining that not only is no language like this in Kate's contracts, but she also has never had implants. (She *has*, however, had digital alterations to her boobs in movie ads.)

Janet Jackson's Breast Gets the Attention of the FCC (Not to Mention the Millions Watching the Super Bowl)

Yes, we are speaking of Nipplegate.

If you didn't see it, you probably heard about it: During the halftime show, while Justin Timberlake and Janet Jackson were singing, Timberlake "accidentally" tore Jackson's top—exposing her breast, which just *happened* to be sporting a perfectly lovely piece of nipple-surrounding jewelry.

It was the Breast Heard Around America.

Scores of people complained about the sexy stunt, or rather "accident." The FCC began cracking down on any and all potentially salacious television. To avoid bringing the wrath of the FCC upon them, TV network honchos cut anything remotely sexy (NBC had a scene from *ER* cut because it showed the breast of an elderly woman). And poor Janet had to pull herself out of the Grammys. (Timberlake, who chivalrously pointed out it was all Jackson's idea, and that he was really, really, really embarrassed, really, did still appear on the show.)

THE SIMPSON FAMILY BREASTS

The Simpson sisters have so much in common: They both sing. They're both blond (well, for now). And they both have BREASTS! And they LOVE them! And they say the SAME (eloquent) THINGS ABOUT THEM! Isn't that just too cute for words?

Let's listen in on their pronouncements about their chests, shall we? (And cue the "We Are Family" soundtrack.)

"I have amazing boobs. I do, I know it. They're not too big, not too small. They're just perfect." —ASHLEE SIMPSON

"I have amazing boobs. They're just perfect."
—JESSICA SIMPSON

But watch out for sibling rivalry. Dear ol' dad Joe Simpson seems a mite too proud of Jessica's older and larger . . . *talents.*

"She just is sexy. If you put her in a T-shirt or you put her in a bustier, she's sexy in both. She's got double Ds! You can't cover those suckers up!"

(Personal note to Ashlee: Not to worry, honey. We're sure Dad thinks your suckers are great too.)

Breaking News: Stars Like Their Breasts!

We interrupt this book to bring you the following news flash: Stars are fond of their breasts, their "girls," their boobs—whatever they call them.

Actually, though, we oversimplify. There are several celebrity schools of thought where breasts are concerned:

Celebrity Breast School #1: My breasts are good! I like them! I really like them!

"I like my body and face, and I love my breasts—my girls."
> —actress SCARLETT JOHANSSON

"Russell, you're not the star! I'm the star! *(pointing at her breasts)* These are the fucking stars!"
> —COURTNEY LOVE to Russell Crowe at the *Vanity Fair* party following the 2001 Academy Awards at which Crowe won the Best Actor Oscar

MAXIM INTERVIEWER: "What do you say to people who think [your breasts] must be fake?"

JENNIFER LOVE HEWITT: "They're not. They're mine, and they've always been mine. *(Giggles loudly)* They're nice, and I like them!"

Celebrity Breast School #2: Other people like my breasts! (Isn't that great!)

"When they're huge, you become very self-conscious . . . I've learned something, though, through my years of pondering and pontificating, and that is: Men love them, and I love that."
> —DREW BARRYMORE

"Hooters are nice. Nice hooters are nice. People think I have nice hooters. I like that!"
> —former Charlie's Angel CHERYL LADD

Celebrity Breast School #3: My breasts are fashionable! Kinda like having a nice handbag!

"When I first got my boobs, I was so insecure. I was 11 years old, with this chest, and it was like, 'Whoa, what is going on?' Then I finally went, 'Wow, what a great accessory to a T-shirt! My T-shirts have never looked so good, how exciting!' "

—JENNIFER LOVE HEWITT

"At school, my boobs were bigger than all my friends' and I was afraid to show them. Now, I feel they make my outfits look better. They're like an accessory."

—JESSICA SIMPSON

Celebrity Breast School #4: My breasts have made me what I am today!

"I had nice boobs before—they were small but nice. . . . Of course I could have them reduced. But then where would I be?"

—CARMEN ELECTRA, talking about how she had her breasts enlarged from 32B to 36DD

Celebrity Breast School #5: My breasts can be such FUN! (For myself and others!)

"I always wanted an orgy to see what it was like, but never got the opportunity. I have good boobs and I know they'd get a lot of attention."

—former *Playboy* model turned actress
JENNY MCCARTHY

Celebrity Breast School #6: Breasts are overrated!

"I'm much more than a pair of breasts. . . . I represent success, hard work and fun."

—PAMELA ANDERSON

"I like being flat. I think it's hot. I never have to wear a bra."

> —PARIS HILTON (in an *Elle* interview. In another interview she mentioned that she had thought about getting implants but was talked out of it by her dad: "Years ago, I asked my dad for a boob job and he said it would cheapen my image." Yes. Cheapen her image.)

NIPPLES 'N' TOES: AN ACTRESS WEIGHS IN

"[My nipples aren't] big or small or objectively that great, but they are to me. For the record, I like my toes just fine. Not as much as my nipples but they're still suck-worthy."

—ACTRESS TERI HATCHER

Celebrity Booty Call: The Bottom Line on Asses— or, Fundamental Thoughts on Fundaments

Why should breasts get all the attention when a lot of stars just love their—or others'—booties? And they aren't loath to share their insights on this all-important body part.

Celebrity Ass Insight #1: Butts are mesmerizing!

"My butt fascinates me. So much so that when I dance, I'm always looking back at it."

> —actress TORI SPELLING

Celebrity Ass Insight #2: Butts are creatively crucial . . . *and* artistically unique!

"I have a special butt. It has special curves and it kinda has its own attitude . . . I think the audience can feel that, and if I were to put someone else's butt in that place, the audience would feel cheated and emotionally insulted."

—actor WILL SMITH—when asked why he did his own underwear scenes in *Enemy of the State*

FAMILY BUTT DOUBLE DOUBLEALERT

It's clearly in their genes—and not in their jeans—as both brothers Owen and Luke Wilson had to use butt doubles for their films. Yes, we're talking double butt doubles.

Owen recent used one in *You, Me and Dupree*—where, apparently, his lack of cheekiness didn't affect his developing a relationship with his co-star Kate Hudson. His *other* co-star, Matt Dillon, also didn't find his butt a problem. "I don't know what's wrong with his butt because I didn't pay any attention to it. I truly don't know what that was all about."

Owen's brother Luke also needed a butt double in his film *My Super Ex-Girlfriend*—and shared the experience. "What they do is they give you photos of different guys' backsides and have you pick one out. I found myself poring over the Polaroids and saying, 'I like that one but it doesn't have quite the pizzazz I want for this scene.' Or, 'This one's good, but it's too muscular.' I've got a little bit of damage back there. As you get a little older, you get little dents and indentations. You want to act cool about it when you eventually say, 'I like this guy's ass.' "

Just in case you're interested: You can earn about $500 for a straight eight-hour day as a butt double . . . and you get more if there's a naked cheek shot involved.

"Charlie Chaplin used his ass better than any other actor. In all of his films his ass is practically the protagonist. For a comic, the ass has incredible importance."

—actor ROBERTO BENIGNI

Celebrity Ass Insight #3: Butts are also private!

"I make sure that they [designers] understand that my booty has to be covered. It's my booty and I feel like when you're walking on the runway, God knows where they're looking. It's not that I feel self-conscious, it's that I feel like my booty should be shown on special occasions, for special people."

—model GISELE BÜNDCHEN

Celebrity Ass Insight #4: Butts make you want to get to know people!

"I'd love to meet Cher and Cyndi Lauper. Their butts are phenomenal."

—JENNIFER LOVE HEWITT

Celebrity Ass Insight #5: But—other body parts are really important too!

"People talk about the heart, the mind, the body. They never talk about the tummy. The tummy tells a lot."

—DREW BARRYMORE

High Cost of Looking Good

It's not easy looking totally photo-fabutastic, you know. Celebrities have to be very, very aware of their appearance what with all those paparazzi, all those red carpet appearances, all those late nights at Bungalow. And, like can-do kind of folks, they make sure that they're ready for the close-up—no matter what the cost!

APPEARANCE-AWARE CELEBRITY	BEAUTY NECESSITY	COST	GOOD INVESTMENT?
Kirstie Alley	Private dance lessons and Jenny Craig meals for weight loss	$10,833 a month for the lessons, a mere $504 a month for Jenny	Well . . . she's trying . . .
Jennifer Aniston	Private Budokon lessons and private Pilates lessons	$6,000 a month and $650 a month, respectively	Our question: Why is the Pilates so cheap compared to the Budokon?
Mariah Carey	Hairdresser and makeup artist on retainer	$8,000 a day	Mariah won't do anything—including walking her dog—without being fully "done"—so it *is* a necessity.
Mariah Carey	68 bottles of Cristal Champagne for bath	$20,400 per bath	At $300 a bottle, it seems better to drink Cristal than soak in it.
Missy Elliott	Naps	$3,000 (for makeup artist to do her makeup while she naps)	Excellent time management!

APPEARANCE-AWARE CELEBRITY	BEAUTY NECESSITY	COST	GOOD INVESTMENT?
Oprah Winfrey	Caviar for special caviar weight-loss diet plan	$2,000 per meal	Not sure how long she stayed on this diet (she didn't look that much thinner . . .). If she stuck to the diet for a year, she'd be spending nearly $2.2 million.
Barbra Streisand	Emergency nail repair	$900—for fingernail and chartered helicopter to fly her from Malibu to fave nail salon in Beverly Hills	How environmentally sound of you, Babs!
Victoria "Posh" Beckham	Teeth whitening	$44,000—at $4,400 per tooth	Posh had always been self-conscious about her teeth (she didn't smile much in Spice Girls pictures). She liked the results so much, her hub "Becks" decided to get the same treatment.
Madonna	Kabbalah water	$49 per day	Well, hey, if it helps "our immune system, digestive system, circulatory system, and . . . every atom of our bodies," it's worth it. We, however, prefer Champagne.

GOOD REASONS FOR SPENDING MONEY ON LOOKING GOOD

Courtney Love explains why it's *vital* for stars to spend big bucks on hairstylists, makeup, surgery, designer diets, and so forth:

"I wanted my anger to be valid, and the only way to do that is to be fairly attractive." —LOVE EXPLAINING WHY SHE HAD
BLEACHED-BLOND HAIR, A NOSE JOB,
AND IS ALWAYS ON A DIET

True Tales of Dubious Celebrity Personal Hygiene

Sadly, no amount of money can totally banish horrible hygiene happenings. Yes, some stars have—or *reputedly* have—rather deplorable personal hygiene or bodily habits.

Larry King: Reportedly Prone to Loud, Noxious Anal Emissions

Not one, not two, but many people report that the great talk show host has the ol' anal air-hose problem. Loud and pungent, too.

One blogger reports sitting next to the great King at a charity barbecue dinner in Sun Valley, Idaho, when the interviewer "leaned left, and beefed right"—directly on his guest. Another professional reports that King's handler had him take frequent fifteen-minute fart breaks during a documentary interview, just to let 'em all loose. For those who need auditory proof of King's anal proclivities: Supposedly, if you listen closely to a recording of King's exclusive Star Jones interview, which aired on June 30, 2005, you can actually hear the celebrity rip one off, at the very end (no pun intended) of the show, just as he's plugging (not literally, also no pun intended) an upcoming guest. At least King is usually considerate about it all. To avoid offending people he's interviewing, we've heard that he politely positions a fan beneath his desk, blowing his noxious fart fallout downwind.

Kimberly Stewart: Accused of Vile Foot Odor

This is controversial: Page Six of the *New York Post* issued an official denial of the story. But the denial was so tepid we can't help but tell it anyway, and let you as the reader draw your own conclusions, as is the journalistic and democratic way. It goes like this: Kimberly Stewart, the daughter of Rocker Rod and, of course, Paris Hilton's best friend, supposedly went to a manicurist at the *W* magazine Oscar Hollywood retreat house for a complete spa treatment. But when she took off her shoes for a pedicure, "her feet stunk so fucking bad that the pedicurist refused to do her toes . . . or anybody else's for the rest of the day," so revolted was the poor spa worker. All of this according to a witness who was supposedly at the scene. But apparently there were some loud complaints from the head connected via a body to the offending feet, as well as from two other heads, resulting in the following "retraction" from the *New York Post:*

> On March 13, 2006, we ran an item stating that a pedicurist at the *W* magazine Oscar Hollywood retreat house refused to do Kimberly Stewart's toes on account of her smelly feet. Stewart swears, along with her parents, Rod and Alana, that we were wrong. Thus, we are convinced that Kimberly did not sit down for a pedicure and that her feet are clean and odorless. Our apologies.

Pete Doherty: Horrible Halitosis

Rocker Pete Doherty allegedly has breath you can probably see, it's so bad. Apparently, it's so awful that lady love
Kate Moss is shelling out $20,000 to fix the problem. Ac-
cording to one source: "The only way to save their romance
is to save his teeth. Pete suffers from terrible halitosis because he rarely brushes his teeth. But he's terrified of losing
her so he's agreed to see the dentist."

Russell Crowe: Reputedly Reeks of B.O.

The actor *Film Threat* called "our favorite wild boor"
fits with his punny accolade, at least according to Joan
Rivers, who reports the phone-throwing boor, or boar, in
this case, smells quite *pungent*.

Purported Celebrity Penile Development Issues—
or, "Is That a Button in Your Pocket or
Are You Just Glad to See Me?"

We've talked about celebrity breasts. What, you may be asking, about celebrity penises?

We know that size, of course, doesn't matter. Besides, almost everyone has a big one. Ask any male and he'll tell you
his is the largest in five counties. Unless you *see* the thing, or
hear from someone who has, you'll probably never know if
he's actually got the more micro version.

But we've been lucky enough to hear about several purported celebrity penile development issues or, to put it
more colloquially, small dick sightings.

Important note: Before you read on, remember, *size
doesn't matter*. So these reported small dick sightings that
we're mentioning below mean absolutely *nothing. Nothing.*

Small Organ Sighting #1

Intelligence Received From: Tara Palmer-Tomkinson
Purported Small Organ Owner: James Blunt

Blunt's big—or small—mistake was reportedly sleeping with Tara's girlfriend Camilla Boler. A steamed Tara revealed to the British press that Blunt was a lousy lover. As she so sweetly put it: "Let's just say the whole experience was small in every sense of the word."

Small Organ Sighting #2

Intelligence Received From: Brittany Murphy
Purported Small Organ Owner: Ashton Kutcher

Poor Ashton. Brittany was on a TV show talking about her ex-boyfriend Ashton's relationship with the then-new older woman in his life, Demi Moore, when she blurted out: "I suppose that the crux of their relationship is that, to him, age doesn't matter and, to her, size doesn't matter."

Get it? Everyone did.

Brittany insisted she was just joking, however, and explained, "My trouble is I talk first and think later. I didn't mean to cause him any offense."

Any offense?

Small Organ Sighting #3

Intelligence Received From: Enrique Iglesias
Purported Small Organ Owner: Enrique Iglesias

No, this is not a typo. Enrique Iglesias himself provided hints as to the size of his perhaps not-so-mighty Spanish poker. The sexy pop singer, who was dating super-sexy tennis star Anna Kournikova at the time, for reasons known only to himself decided to discourse publicly on condoms and suggested that he might be sponsoring a line of special penis covers. He reportedly said: "I can never find extra-

A TRIFECTA OF NAUSEATINGLY CUTESY-PIE EUPHEMISMS

Some female celebrities don't want to call a spade a spade—or, more precisely, a tit a tit. They'd rather use a totally adorable word to cover the naughty bits.

Our favorites:

1. Jennifer Garner calls her breasts her "biscuits."

The actress and wife of Ben Affleck told *In Style* magazine that she's proud of her chest (we assume that's what she's talking about . . .): "My sisters and I were all endowed with biscuits—that's what I call them. Sometimes when I'm on the *Alias* set and the guys are setting up a camera shot, I'll ask: 'Is this a biscuit shot?' and they'll say: 'Yeah' so I know."

2. Jessica Simpson calls her "bikini area" (to use another less cute euphemism) her "wawa."

ROLLING STONE INTERVIEWER: "Wax or shave for summertime?"
JESSICA SIMPSON: "I'm a baby, so I shave. And I guess it's weird, but being a celebrity, I just don't like to have other people see my . . . you know . . . wawa."

3. And, finally, an oldie but goodie about a non–body part. Kathie Lee Gifford (remember her? She was Kelly Ripa before Kelly was) wrote in her autobiography, *I Can't Believe I Said That*, that she calls something (we're not sure what . . .) "wuggies":

"I change my hairstyle every day for the show, I'm fastidious and vain about my nails and teeth and grooming and makeup, but a perfect body, forget it. Dust to dust, wuggies to wuggies."

small condoms, and I know it's really embarrassing for people—you know, from experience."

Many people quite reasonably took this to mean that the singer was referring to himself in terms of condom size, and hence, penile size. But now the Spanish star insists his remarks not only were misunderstood, but were hurting his relationship with Kournikova, saying: "It's not true and hurtful to me and my girlfriend."

So if it's not true, why does he buy extra-small? For party favors? To helpfully hand out to smaller, less well endowed friends? There's a mystery here.

SOME STARS LIKE BIG BOATS

Juliette Lewis explains her love for large endowments poetically, using lovely *nautical* imagery: "Visually the size of the boat is wonderful, really pleasing on the eye."

3

CELEBRITY BEHAVIOR

I T's ALL WELL AND good to have great breasts—or butts—or penises (as the case may be), but there's more to being a celebrity than mere toned (or large) body parts.

In other words, there are many people with absolutely stupendous breasts or butts who are *not* celebrities. So what else does it take to make a celebrity?

Talent?

Maybe, but not usually.

We're thinking of another word. *Behavior.* To be a celebrity you've got to *act* like a celebrity. You've got to be rude, dominant, domineering, arrogant, nasty—all those adjectives young people aspire to.

The Celebrity Etiquette Awards

Celebrities are, sans doubt, etiquette experts. They have to be. They're always meeting people, greeting people, shaking hands, air kissing, etc., etc., etc.

Sadly, the media focus all too often on the negatives about celebrity behavior. Columns and blogs talk about drink-throwing, wardrobe malfunctions, glassy-eyed stumbling, celebrity feuds, and the like, but don't mention the genteel and civilized behavior so many celebs exhibit.

We think this is patently unfair. In an effort to remedy this situation, we herewith present the "Etties"—awarding celebrities for their moments of true politesse.

The "Welcome Wagon" Award goes to . . . Shannen Doherty

You don't have to bother introducing yourself when warm and friendly Shannen is around. A perfect example of her grace: When she saw fellow actress and new neighbor Molly Ringwald at a neighborhood party, she immediately made her feel at home with a warm and hearty "I know who *you* are. You don't live here, you *rent.*"

The "Hello, I Must Be Going" Award goes to . . . Nicky Hilton

The famous-for-being-rich-and-having-a-sister Nicky Hilton (oops—she also is a "designer" and a "hotelier"—how could we forget?) demonstrated her affable charm when at a fancy-dancy Hollywood birthday party. She spotted actress Mischa Barton, but didn't have the time to stop and chat, as she was apparently eager to go have a schmooze with her pal Rick Salomon (who sold a tape of himself having sex with her sister Paris). But did Nicky just pass her by without acknowledging Mischa's presence? Of *course* not! Even in her rush, Nicky managed a second or two to politely make it clear she remembered her by saying, "What is that fat pig doing here?"

The "Class Act" Award goes to . . . Janice Dickinson

Talk about someone who really knows how to break the ice! Model and reality show host Dickinson threw herself into host Ryan Seacrest's lap while on his syndicated *On-Air*

TV show—and coyly cracked, "I feel something rising." Sadly, Seacrest's producers didn't share her clever sense of humor and asked her to leave. (Reports say that Dickinson's manager summed it up by saying: "He's a big wuss! These West Coast guys can't handle the alpha dog.")

The "Grace Under Pressure" Award goes to . . . Kelly Clarkson

When Clarkson—shortly after winning *American Idol*—met her own idol, Mariah Carey, she managed to act completely natural and totally unaffected. Instead of opting for empty flattery, she instead said exactly what was on her mind: "I think I'm gonna puke." (We are happy to report that the words are the only thing that came out of her mouth.)

The "Why Can't They All Be Like Kiefer?" Award goes to . . . Kiefer Sutherland

Now here's a class act if we ever saw one! He and some pals were drinking for seven hours—generally having a fine old time—when he saw a Christmas tree in a hotel lobby. Said Christmas tree was bringing him down, man, so he decided that he just had to trash it. But the parfit gentil Kiefer *asked* first, saying to a hotel staff member: "I hate that fucking Christmas tree! The tree *has* to come down. I'm smashing it. Can I pay for it?" Said the obliging staffer: "I'm absolutely sure you can, sir."

Celebrity Fears and Phobias

Many celebrities, like the rest of us, are prone to phobias.

There are the normal phobias, such as fear of flying (or aviophobia), which afflicts such people as Aretha Franklin,

Cher, Muhammad Ali, and John Madden. And there's fear of the dark (scotophobia), which afflicts actress Joan Collins and novelist Anne Rice; fear of confined spaces (claustrophobia), which afflicts Woody Allen; and the flip side, fear of wide, open spaces (agoraphobia), which afflicts Kim Basinger.

But some celebrities have phobias that are a little . . . *different*. . . .

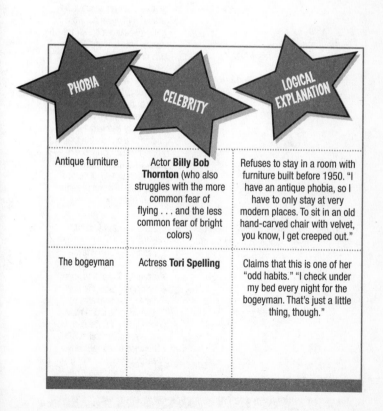

PHOBIA	CELEBRITY	LOGICAL EXPLANATION
Antique furniture	Actor **Billy Bob Thornton** (who also struggles with the more common fear of flying . . . and the less common fear of bright colors)	Refuses to stay in a room with furniture built before 1950. "I have an antique phobia, so I have to only stay at very modern places. To sit in an old hand-carved chair with velvet, you know, I get creeped out."
The bogeyman	Actress **Tori Spelling**	Claims that this is one of her "odd habits." "I check under my bed every night for the bogeyman. That's just a little thing, though."

PHOBIA	CELEBRITY	LOGICAL EXPLANATION
Butterflies	Actress **Nicole Kidman**	Phobia began as a child in Australia. "Sometimes when I would come home from school the biggest butterfly or moth you'd ever seen would be just sitting on our front gate. I would climb over the fence, crawl around to the side of the house—anything to avoid having to go through the front gate. I have tried to get over it. I walked into the big butterfly cage at the American Museum of Natural History and had the butterflies on me, but that didn't work. I jump out of planes, I could be covered in cockroaches, I do all sorts of things, but I just don't like the feel of butterflies' bodies."
Clowns	Actor **Johnny Depp** (also rapper **P. Diddy Combs**)	Developed this fear after buying a clown painting by serial killer John Wayne Gacy . . . and after Gacy was executed. "Something about the painted face, the fake smile . . . There always seemed to be a darkness lurking just under the surface, a potential for real evil." Summed up more briefly: "Fear . . . Fear . . . Utter fear. Clowns! Clowns scare me."

PHOBIA	CELEBRITY	LOGICAL EXPLANATION
Cows	Country singer **Lyle Lovett**	Having been trampled and mauled by a bull in 2002, Lyle appears to have a relatively reasonable phobia.
Feet	Actress **Tara Reid**	"I hate feet. They freak me out. I don't like my own feet, either. There's something about feet that's creepy. I just think they're dirty. I hate any part of the body that can stink that bad."
Germans	Actor **Christian Slater**	When arrested in 1997 for a drug- and alcohol-induced brawl, made statements to the arresting officers (according to the arrest report): "The Germans are all coming and they will kill us."
Houseplants	Actress **Christina Ricci**	Confessed to this very particular form of botanophobia in a British *Esquire* article: "They are dirty. If I have to touch one, after already being repulsed by the fact that there is a plant indoors, then it just freaks me out."

PHOBIA	CELEBRITY	LOGICAL EXPLANATION
Komodo dragons	**Billy Bob Thornton** (again)	Says that these are what terrifies him most (even more than antique furniture). His explanation: "Dragons are evil. Komodo dragons have this horribly toxic bacteria in their mouths. When they bite you, you go blind. Then they all gather around you and watch you die like they are watching television. They don't eat you right away. They wait till you die. Then they eat you."
Pigs	Actor **Orlando Bloom**	Reportedly had panic attack during the filming of *Kingdom of Heaven* when a small porker escaped onto the set.
Sloppiness and odd numbers	Soccer star **David Beckham**	Not just your basic neat freak, but rather an "ataxophobic," or one who fears disorder. Everything in his house is color-coordinated; he's been known to pick clothing based on the color of his furniture; refrigerator contents are perfectly lined up. Said his wife Victoria (aka the former Posh Spice): "Everything has to match in the house. If there are three cans of diet Coke he'd throw one away rather than having three because it's uneven."

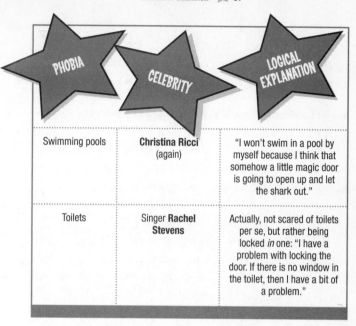

PHOBIA	CELEBRITY	LOGICAL EXPLANATION
Swimming pools	**Christina Ricci** (again)	"I won't swim in a pool by myself because I think that somehow a little magic door is going to open up and let the shark out."
Toilets	Singer **Rachel Stevens**	Actually, not scared of toilets per se, but rather being locked *in* one: "I have a problem with locking the door. If there is no window in the toilet, then I have a bit of a problem."

The Naomi Campbell Anger Management Activities Chart—or, Why You Might Not Ever Want to Work For, Go Out With, or Generally Get Within 15 Feet of Naomi

As any celebrity-watcher knows, Naomi Campbell, of course, is the queen of anger management issues. Who among us has not thrilled to hear of yet another Naomi rage-out?

Back in 2000, Naomi Campbell pleaded guilty to hitting her personal assistant with a cell phone and was ordered to take anger management classes. Have those classes worked? Is Naomi a kinder, gentler person who knows to count to ten before acting out?

Just take a wild guess . . . then skip to the next page to begin perusing our handy Naomi Campbell Anger Management Activities Chart, which details some episodes that allegedly happened after those helpful classes.

Naomi Campbell Wannabes: A Few Angry Celebrities

There are celebrities other than Naomi Campbell who have . . . well, let's just kindly say, "global temper problems." Here are a few, rated on a scale of 1 to 5—with 5 representing total Naomi-dom and 1 being a mere poseur.

Angry Person: Model May Anderson
Angry Altercation: Got into a bit of a tizzy on a plane and allegedly slapped a flight attendant on a flight from Amsterdam to Miami. Was charged with assault and refused entry into the United States.
Naomi Campbell Anger Management Scale: **1.** Only one slapping? Nothing thrown? She has a *long* way to go before she reaches the heights of Naomi-angerdom.

Angry Person: Singer Frank Sinatra
Angry Altercation: In Sands Hotel office, ripped telephone out of wall, broke windows and set room on fire—because color of phone clashed with his sweater.
Naomi Campbell Anger Management Scale: **2.** Gets points for throwing things and fashion awareness, but can't rate higher because only *inanimate* objects were involved.

Angry Person: Singer Grace Jones
Angry Altercation: While Jones was on his talk show, host Russell Harty turned away to speak to other guests. She punched him.

WHEN	WHERE	WHAT REPORTEDLY SET HER OFF	HOW SHE ALLEGEDLY "ACTED OUT"	ANYTHING THROWN?	FALLOUT
10/06	Therapist's Westminster, London, residence	Uncertain	Allegedly scratched her drug counselor	No	A spokesman for Campbell said, "There has been a misunderstanding."
7/06	Outside of ex-boyfriend Badr Jafar's home in London at 3:30 A.M.	Wanted her belongings from ex-boyfriend	When bf wouldn't let her in began shouting very loudly—waking up the neighbors. Wound up in the arms of London's Metropolitan Police after they received "reports of a woman causing a disturbance."	Unknown	Held for "breach of peace"; released by police after several hours.

WHEN	WHERE	WHAT REPORTEDLY SET HER OFF	HOW SHE ALLEGEDLY "ACTED OUT"	ANYTHING THROWN?	FALLOUT
7/06	Tuscan Riviera, on $2.8 million yacht belonging to boyfriend Badr Jafar, a prince from Dubai	The appetizers: tomato, mozzarella and dried ham served with a local white wine	Yelled at chef who responded with "colorful Tuscan dialect," according to the *Sun*. She, in turn, responded by breaking things—antiques, lights, china, glasses . . . pretty much anything at hand. Said a man at the harbor where the yacht was docked: "All hell seemed to break loose. All you could hear was shouting and screaming in English. There was the sound of plates being broken. . . . Some of the crew later said the kitchen was a complete mess and the curtains and cushions had all been ripped apart."	Yes: plates, glasses, lights, etc.	Allegedly caused $54,000 of damage; broke up with boyfriend (see p. 53); Campbell is suing the *Sun*, the paper that reported this, saying it never happened.

3/06	Her Park Avenue penthouse	Couldn't find her Chip & Pepper jeans	Accused maid Ana Scolavino of stealing the missing $200 jeans; bashed maid's head with BlackBerry, yelling "You fucking bitch." After maid called cops, told staff to tell cops that the maid had hurt herself falling. Told cops she had no idea what they were there for, showed them flip-phone, not BlackBerry, as proof that she'd done nothing. Cops cuffed her—even though an Oprah Winfrey camera crew was there to shoot her for a cooking segment. Naomi hid cuffs under white fur poncho—and asked if she could ride in her own car and allow staffers to fix her bangs. Both requests were denied.	Yes; jewel-encrusted BlackBerry	Charged with assault; she denied allegation: "She is sadly mistaken if she thinks she can extract money from me by concocting lies by recycling old stories. . . . I have asked my lawyer to look into filing both theft and extortion charges against her." But in January 2007, she pleaded guilty and was sentenced to five days of community service, two days of anger management courses, and payment of her ex-maid's medical bills.
2/06	British Airways London-L.A. flight	Didn't like service—which got her all het up about her assistant's work	Complained that assistant hadn't gotten dresses sent to wherever they should have been sent; assistant responded by yelling that she was quitting. Escalated into yelling match at which point passengers complained to the flight attendant, who was going to get the pilot to intervene. Stopped yelling then and both sulked in silence.	No	Assistant quit.

WHEN	WHERE	WHAT REPORTEDLY SET HER OFF	HOW SHE ALLEGEDLY "ACTED OUT"	ANYTHING THROWN?	FALLOUT
1/06	Her Park Avenue penthouse	Assistant couldn't find her Stella McCartney jeans.	When jeans were not located, hit assistant on back of head with hand, yelled, swore, and threatened to have her arrested for stealing clothes.	No	Assistant made formal claim of harassment, but couldn't press abuse charges due to lack of visible injury.
10/05	U2 concert at Madison Square Garden, New York	Security guard asked her to get off barrier separating the band from the audience.	When asked to get off barrier, told guard that he was a fucking asshole; told him to go fuck himself and get the fuck away from her—then spat in his face. A senior Garden official came over to calm things down, explaining that it was against Garden policy to allow people to sit on the barrier and that spitting in someone's face was cause for ejection; she told the official to get the fuck out of her face—adding that she'd like to see him try to kick her out.	No—but she did spit a nice loogie.	Wasn't ejected from concert; no police report filed

8/05	Hotel Eden, Rome	Italian actress Yvonne Scio was wearing same dress as her.	Kicked and punched Scio when she saw her in the dress; Scio wound up at San Giacomo hospital with split lip and cuts on face.	Just fists	Scio filed police complaint and hired lawyer to possibly pursue civil lawsuit. Naomi's agent said: "Supermodel Naomi Campbell has been mistakenly dragged into a potential drama in Rome after an actress and longtime acquaintance, Yvonne Scio, made claims of a dispute between the two. Naomi made it clear that there had been a disagreement between the two in which she told Ms. Scio she was very disappointed with her behavior and that she should go."
2/05	Carnival parade, Brazil	Friend ticked her off.	Got in argument with friend, flipped friend the bird and yelled, "Fuck you." Was upset that other people were laughing about it.	No	Naomi's feelings were hurt.

WHEN	WHERE	WHAT REPORTEDLY SET HER OFF	HOW SHE ALLEGEDLY "ACTED OUT"	ANYTHING THROWN?	FALLOUT
11/04	Her Park Avenue penthouse	Assistant Amie Castaldo told her she was quitting.	Blew up when Castaldo hired "wrong" hairstylist, prompting Amie to quit. Responded by biting Castaldo's lip, head-butting her, pulling her hair, throwing cell phone at head and calling her a "fucking worthless bitch."	Yes— cell phone	Castaldo's doctor filed report saying the injuries could have occurred "no other way than traumatic incident." Naomi's spokesperson issued statement saying "She categorically denies wild accusations by Amie Castaldo."
8/04	Her Park Avenue penthouse	Maid shoved her after Naomi "got in her face and was yelling" at her.	Yelled at maid who then shoved her; slapped maid and threw her purse out the door. Cops were called.	Maid's purse	Police said "just a violation," no further investigation needed. Naomi's lawyer said: "Miss Campbell vigorously disputes the version of these events that is being presented by Miss Burton. It was Miss Burton who precipitated these events, and it is Miss Burton who apparently hopes to capitalize on the incident that she created."

Naomi Campbell Anger Management Scale: **3.** Landing a punch earns Jones several points; however, nothing was thrown and she didn't follow up with any "fucks," "bitches," or the like.

Angry Person: Singer Björk
Angry Altercation: Got a tad upset during filming of director Lars von Trier's *Dancer in the Dark.* Used teeth to tear chunk from the director's shirt, then stormed off the set. (She returned four days later.)
Naomi Campbell Anger Management Scale: **4.** Using teeth is a nice, creative, Naomi-esque touch.

Angry Person: Rapper Foxy Brown
Angry Altercation: Allegedly hit manicurist with (pause for dramatic effect) a cell phone! Manicurists claim that she assaulted one of them with said cell phone after she walked out of the salon without paying for a pedicure. Brown's lawyer claims that she wanted both a manicure and pedicure, but didn't get her feet done—and the manicurists locked her in and demanded payment for the nonexistent pedicure. But she wound up pleading guilty—and was required to serve three years probation and take anger management classes. She was later kicked out of anger management classes . . . for being too angry.
Naomi Campbell Anger Management Scale: **5.** A cell phone? And getting booted from anger management classes? Foxy, hon, you're thisclose to being Naomi!

Puerile Celebrity Bickering: The Stupidest and Most Childish Celebrity Feuds

Some celebrities—let us amend that, most celebrities—remain perpetually young. No, we are not speaking of Botox. We are speaking of attitude.

And, while we are at it, no, we are not speaking of child-like innocence. We are speaking of behavior worthy of a snotty kindergartner—one who has pushed his or her classmate down the slide. Backwards.

Here, then, are some of the most notoriously stupid celebrity feuds, coupled with absolutely preadolescent behavior.

Stevie Cuts in Line—and Jeremy Gets Mad!

It happened on June 7, 2006, after Sean Combs's party at the Pink Elephant. Entourage star Jeremy Piven was standing in a line for the bathroom at the after-hours club Bungalow 8, telling a bystander how he wanted to "score with chicks," when actor Stephen Dorff (of *Blade* and *Cecil B. DeMented*) did the unthinkable.

He CUT AHEAD of Jeremy in line.

According to a *New York Post* source, the ensuing dialogue was "very high school." We beg to differ. We'd say it was more junior high school, or maybe advanced elementary school:

> PIVEN: "Yo, what are you doing? You know you don't need to cut the line!"
> DORFF: "I can do what I want!"
> PIVEN: "No you can't!"
> DORFF: "Yes I can!"
> PIVEN: "You're a has-been!"

DORFF: "At least I am a movie star—you're only on TV! Cable TV!"

At this last comment, Piven began screaming expletives, and security guards were called in. According to a witness, Jeremy was shoved into a bathroom by guards and soon left. Dorff, stuck in a standing-room-only section, stayed for most of the night, "telling anyone who would listen, 'I am going to kick Jeremy Piven's ass.'" Eventually, he too left, arriving at Scores West where he reportedly announced to the strippers there: "I'm a movie star—you should want to sleep with me."

Brandon Makes Rude Comments About Lindsay's Snatch!

What better way to get back at someone than to criticize their vagina? This thought evidently passed through the apparently underdeveloped inner brain portion of Brandon "I'm Famous 'Cause My Dad's a Billionaire and I Dated Paris Hilton" Davis, who made the following comment concerning Lindsay Lohan: "Lindsay Lohan is a firecrotch, she has freckles coming out of her vagina, and her clitoris is seven feet long." There was more, much more, but it all pretty much followed this tone and general level of discourse. The key word, repeated over and over again, was "firecrotch."

After several witty addenda to this theme, the celebrity billionaire's boy made a somewhat abject apology: "What started out as a joke got completely carried away and I am horrified at the words that came out of my mouth. I consider Lindsay a friend and I hope she accepts my sincere apology for my reprehensible actions last week."

But it's so tough to let go of a clever theme. . . . A short time later, the abashed young billionaire seized a mike at

Paris Hilton's CD debut party and shouted, "I wrote a special new song called 'Firecrotch,' and it's for Lindsay Lohan!"

Ah, the clever witticisms of youth.

Eminem Calls Moby a *Girl*!

Eminem, currently and perhaps justly not recognized by many as a man with a cutting, rapier-like wit, got a chance to exercise such after the 2001 Grammy Awards when gay rights activists picketed his performance—and when Moby added that Eminem was "very good at what he does, but he's also a homophobe, a racist, and a misogynist."

Eminem took his revenge in his next single, "Without Me." Perhaps not understanding the longer words Moby used, Eminem confined himself to easier words and concepts, as befits a perhaps somewhat simpler mind. In short, he called Moby *gay, bald, aging and unpopular*, all but the last words of one or two syllables. Then at the MTV Video awards, he told a booing audience he was distracted by that "Moby *girl*." Yes, he actually called Moby a *girl*, and evidently meant this to be a stinging insult.

Eminem added that he could "hit a man with glasses," and wittily rejoined that Moby was not only a girl but a "36-year-old balding fag."

J Lo Tries to Ruin Britney's Party by Holding Her Own on the Same Day!

The transgression was horrific. Multimillionaire singer/star J Lo was *actually asked to contribute to the goody bags* for the launch of Britney's new restaurant (NYLA—in the Dylan Hotel in New York). So incensed was the good singer in being asked to *give* (and not take) something that she got the ultimate revenge: she threw a party *on the same night*—forcing mutual friends to reveal their loyalties to either her or Britney by picking between the two.

Very nasty behavior; like scheduling your third-grade birthday party on the same day as your ex–best friend's.

Lindsay Makes Jessica Cry and Then Says She Wants to Beat Her Up

It started when Jessica Simpson didn't do what most mothers say you should always do: say thank you.

Jessica didn't after Lindsay Lohan had sent over a round of drinks to her and Brett Ratner at the Dime. We don't know if she and Brett forgot, or they were being nasty. And we do know that after waiting and still not being thanked Lohan went over and confronted Jessica. She said:

> "What's the matter? When your sister is around, you can talk shit about me, but now that Ashlee's not here, what are you going to do? C'mon! I'm 19 and you're 25. Say something, you coward!"

Simpson burst into tears, telling Lohan she didn't want to create a scene. But Lindsay didn't care; in fact, she got even more angry. She said: "Let's go outside then, you and me. Alone. I don't need to embarrass you. I'm not causing a scene. You think I care? Step outside! Let's go."

Billy Says Al Is Short and Fat and That He Wishes He Were a Cowboy

To clarify, Bill O'Reilly is the one wishing he were a cowboy, but it seems to us that he wishes that Al Franken was one too. He also noted that Al Franken was short and fat.

The cowboy thing seems to us to be a little off. . . .

The Billy-Al feud began when TV interviewer and pun-

dit of sorts Bill O'Reilly was called a liar by comedian/
commentator Al Franken, and challenged him. But as Bill
challenged, it all got a little, well, *weird*. Like Bill sort of
wanted to *shoot* Al, *dressed up in a cowboy costume:*

> "And you know, as I said at the top of the broadcast,
> somebody calls you a liar to your face, you don't just
> laugh that off. Okay, that's—that's an insult. In the
> Old West, that would have got you shot. See, in the
> Old West—and I would have loved to have been
> in the Old West—Al and I would have just had a
> little—a little shootout, you know? We would have
> went out on Wilshire Avenue, and six-shooters [*sic*].
> Now, he's a much smaller target than I am—about
> four-foot-eleven, but he's wider. And it would have
> been, you know, Clint Eastwood time. I would have
> had the serape, would have given my squint, and I
> would have put a bullet right between his head [*sic*].
> Would have been wrong, would have been wrong.
> But it was the Old West, and I would not have
> known any better. So I wouldn't have been account-
> able because I would not have known any better.
> Now I do. Now, in 2003, that would have been
> wrong."

Yes, it would have been wrong. We're glad that Bill
O'Reilly is advanced enough to see this. Shooting people
who call you names is not very *mature* behavior.

How Celebrities Cope with Autograph Seekers

For some reason, many people get an almost orgasmic thrill
out of holding a piece of paper with the ink signature of

someone famous—such as the third runner-up on *American Idol.* Just imagine the thrill for yourself; sitting there, holding that precious signature and knowing it's yours, all yours. Forever until you die. Yours.

Wow.

For another reason, many celebrities have an almost insane aversion to giving their fans this orgasmic thrill; preferring that their fans get their orgasms in other, more natural (or for that matter more unnatural) ways that importantly do not involve the celebrity's personal participation. Bruce Willis and Demi Moore are famous for their snarling refusals; but they're getting tiresome, so here are some of the *other* worst autograph offenders:

Star: Annie Lennox

Rude Behavior to Autograph Seeker: When she was approached by an unusually handsome autograph seeker, Annie allegedly snubbed him and rudely said: "I just want a quiet night. Please leave me alone and *get a life.*" (our italics)

Comment: Now for the fun addendum to this story of Lennox's alleged rude behavior—the handsome autograph seeker she told to "get a life" actually has quite a life, arguably a bigger one than hers, in that he was none other than superstar actor Orlando Bloom. According to a source (as reported to the *Daily Star*):

It was like watching a car crash unfold. Nobody could understand why she was being so rude to Orlando of all people. It was difficult to believe she didn't know who he was. He's been in almost every blockbuster this year. But it turns out she genuinely thought he was an unusually good-looking fan. She must have been living under a rock for the past few years.

Annie was said to be *very* upset about her mistake—it is one thing, of course, to snub a regular person who can't affect your career and is genetically inferior to you and your fellow stars; it's another to snub a real bonafide celebrity, and so she *raced* over to apologize. She gave Orlando her autograph, and he gave her a kiss on the cheek. One observer reported, "She was bright red when he smooched her." Of course, Annie later completely denied the story, writing on her official website: "We had a really nice two-minute chat. There's not a shred of truth in any of it. Bizarre. Why would anyone invent a piece of nonsense like that?"

Star: Actor Leonardo DiCaprio
Rude Behavior to Autograph Seeker: When a fan approached the great actor asking for an autograph, the multimillionaire suggested a cash payment was in order. The amount is unknown to us.

Comment: Alas, all too typical behavior. DiCaprio was not much classier than those cash-strapped mostly has-been celebrities who go to shows and charge for their signatures. Historical footnote: Cary Grant, the movie star idol of the '30s, '40s, '50s, and '60s, was a pioneer in this sort of thing: when asked for his autograph, the handsome, debonair, and wealthy star would charge 50 cents for children, $1 for adults—and up to $2 for adults who looked rich.

Star: Lindsay Lohan
Rude Behavior to Autograph Seeker: A fan approached Lindsay Lohan, who was at a Beverly Hills Four Seasons

getting a manicure, and asked if she would sign her name. Lindsay snapped: "Wait until I'm finished"— then snuck out a side door without signing.

Comment: How rude can you get? It gets worse when you learn more of the facts: 1) The woman asking for the autograph didn't want it for herself; she was carrying a poster of Lohan that she wanted signed for her young niece. (Note that Lohan probably had received a royalty payment from the sale of the poster.) 2) Lindsay kept the woman waiting for her

Autograph Collector magazine has rated these stars the worst of Hollywood autograph-givers:

1. Cameron Diaz
   (she has a habit of lecturing autograph seekers on how stupid autograph collecting is)
2. Bruce Willis
3. Demi Moore
4. Tobey Maguire
5. Alan Alda
6. Halle Berry
7. Winona Ryder
8. Teri Hatcher
9. Joaquin Phoenix
10. Russell Crowe

for *40 minutes* before sneaking out. 3) The little niece was a destitute orphan, friendless and handicapped, confined to a wheelchair. (1 and 2 are true; 3 *could* have been true, for all Lindsay knew.)

So Big Deal, You're a Fan of Mine; Get Out of the Frickin' Way

Fans love their stars, and stars love their fans. Some stars, that is.

Other stars have a love/hate relationship with their fan base that usually lists rather alarmingly toward the hate side of things—or toward contempt, disgust, loathing, or any number of concepts that pretty basically denote absolute *detestation*.

Sometimes it's hard to fathom why these stars are so nasty. It's one thing to get peckish at an overagitated fan interrupting your salade niçoise for the ninth time begging for yet another autograph; it's another to get *nasty* at a perfectly reasonable fan who is doing something that is, appropriately enough, perfectly reasonable.

As a test case of celebrity behavior, below we have put you, the reader, in the celebrities' rather large shoes and inflated heads. You can see how *you* would behave in a similar circumstance toward a fan (or fans); and then check your answer against what the celebrity actually did.

(Cheaters: Please note that #3 is always the celebrity answer.)

You are **PIERCE BROSNAN,** fresh from a starring role as James Bond, and flush with the millions you've earned for essentially just looking relatively handsome and occasionally leering out a line or two. You are at Seattle's W Hotel bar and the bartender jokingly asks you how you want your martini. You say:

1. "Shaken, not stirred," just like in all the movies, recognizing that although you've heard this 1,000 times before, the bartender hasn't, and it'll give him a little thrill to say, "*I served a martini to James Bond!*"
2. "Thanks, but I think I'll have a screwdriver instead."
3. "If I hear that bloody line one more time, I'm going to punch someone's lights out!"

You are a rapper with the charmingly *clever* name of BUSTA RHYMES. You are at a concert in Denmark and just as you are about to rap you notice a man in a funny-looking chair in the front row who is not standing up along with the rest of the crowd in excited anticipation of hearing your quasi-musical genius. You . . .

1. begin rapping anyway.
2. nod at the man, assume he's tired, and begin rapping anyway.
3. shout at the audience and say: "I didn't come from the other end of the world to see people sit on their ass!" Then you yell again and order the audience, "Everybody—get up!"

Note: The man who remained seated unfortunately was unable to comply with Busta's rather vigorous exhortations to rise, as he was handicapped—the funny-looking chair he was sitting in was a wheelchair.

You are ex–Partridge Family singer DAVID CASSIDY (and incidentally you are not exactly a self-made man as you have had the advantage of having a rich producer father and a famous millionaire actress mother). You are doing a concert in Cardiff, Wales, not exactly the garden spot of the Planet Earth, but hey, most of these people here at the concert can't afford to live in Ibiza or Hawaii. They're *stuck* in Cardiff, Wales. As you look over the crowd and reflect on where you are, you think to yourself that Cardiff, Wales, is a real dump. Then you:

1. politely keep that thought to yourself and begin the concert.

2. make a little white lie and say something like "Glad to be in the wonderful city of Cardiff."

3. look at the crowd, maybe snarl a little, and say: "I don't know how you live here without slitting your wrists."

Note: Fortunately, David Cassidy had an expert PR rep who explained his unfortunate comments with the *perfectly understandable* excuse that "the weather was getting to him, and he was exhausted."

You are CLAY AIKEN, the *very talented* runner-up on *American Idol*. During a Christmas-season concert in New Jersey, your performance has so far been aided by the wonderful performance of students of the Clearview Regional High School Vocal Ensemble. You:

1. thank the students and agree to appear with them at their high school.

2. thank the students and pay the school a $500 honorarium for their performance, as agreed upon beforehand.

3. verbally berate the students, allegedly stiff the school the $500 honorarium, skip an autograph session, and have the 2003 Teacher of the Year booted from the show when she stands up for the kids.

You are pop singer JENNIFER LOPEZ, and you are appearing at the eighth annual Wango Tango pop festival in California. Most of your audience consists of girls in the age range of 12 years (plus or minus two or three years). Understanding your audience, and realizing that you are, for reasons known only to God, something of a role model, you appear on stage in:

1. faded jeans and a red and white fitted sweater.
2. miniskirt, cropped turtleneck, and leather vest.
3. a shredded white shirt over a black T-shirt with the words FUCK IT!

Celebrity Bosses from Dante's Ninth Circle

Some of the worst bosses in the world (and quite probably the universe) are famous celebrities. Naomi Campbell, featured earlier in this book, is easily the single most *unlikely* human on the planet to be voted "Nicest Celebrity Boss of the Year." She has the unfortunate habit of letting cell phones (and other nearby portable objects) fly when she gets upset with her employees, which happens frequently. It wouldn't be so bad except that Campbell apparently has a fairly good throwing arm and very often manages to connect the thrown object with her employees' heads and other sensitive body parts.

But short of throwing things, many celebrities treat their employees like trash in other interesting ways, which we shall explore here in our examination of celebrity bosses from medieval versions of Hell, in which we examine the different types of abusive employers.

Diana Ross
Type of Abusive Employer: Eye-contact avoidance obsessive

Quite possibly something of an overarching egomaniac, the diva singer has demanded that backstage lackeys never make eye contact with her while they are prepping for her concerts. The reason, we conjecture, is related to size of ego; it is a superiority thing. Looking at a celebrity with one's eyes shows that one is a human being and not a minion. Celebrities such as Ross often prefer minions.

Jennifer Lopez

Type of Abusive Employer: Eye-contact avoidance obsessive and general abusive

Another of the bizarre "no looking with the eyes, please" bunch. Lopez reportedly yelled at a contractor working at her house for daring to make eye contact with her. Unlike Diana Ross, however, she gave the contractor a helpful hint: She told him to look at her shoes while talking to her.

There's more . . . but we don't know exactly *what.*

A tantalizing snippet comes from an article in the New York *Daily News* and it hints that life is not easy at Chez Lopez, at least if one is an underling. Apparently, acclaimed filmmaker D. A. Pennebaker filmed a behind-the-scenes documentary on the making of a Jennifer Lopez CD, and "sources say Sony execs were thrilled with his film, but that J Lo hated the sound of her voice and scenes showing her abusing her employees." What kind of "abusing" was she doing? Sitting on them and smothering them with her rather ample and now presumably *floppy* backside? We can only *imagine.*

Marlo Thomas

Type of Abusive Employer: Potty-mouthed

Marlo Thomas was the perky young '60s ingenue on the cute TV show *That Girl,* now seen on reruns. She later married Phil Donahue, the father of "serious" talk shows like Oprah's. If the book written by Thomas's (former) butler is anywhere near the truth, working for Marlo Thomas was no piece of angel food cake. Apparently, Marlo was a particular stickler for proper foods for her guests at luncheons, etc., and had a habit of admonishing her butler if cookies or other such desirable foods were not present, or if other undesirable foods *were* present. Below are two such admonishments, helpfully recollected by her butler:

Marlo Thomas Admonishment #1 (*nonpresence of cookies version*): "Noooooo coooooookies!!! No fucking cookies! I have guests who want cookies! Just what do you expect me to tell them! You fucking fool! No cookies because you didn't bother to check! And you're supposed to be in charge! You go and tell my guests that you are so stupid you forgot the cookies!"

Marlo Thomas Admonishment #2 (*presence of undesirable cold cuts version*): "How dare you serve cold cuts in my house. It's just so low-class and common. And white bread and pickles! And my God, *meat* lasagna!!! Fucker, you've done it again."

Claudia Schiffer
Type of Abusive Employer: Lawsuit junkie

Some people, model Claudia Schiffer among them evidently, take themselves *very, very* seriously. If you work for them and cross the line, watch out for incoming attorneys. In cook Sophie Mitchell's case, the results were disastrous. The cook, who was then working for Schiffer, decided to come out with a cookbook. For the book jacket she used a quote from a letter the model had written to her mother: "We love Sophie and everyone loves her cooking too." Unfortunately, *Mitchell did not ask Schiffer for permission to use the quote with Schiffer's name.*

For Schiffer, this was tantamount to a nuclear bomb. The good and well-heeled model not only protested, she got the book withdrawn from publication. And recovered damages. The cook ended up in bankruptcy.

Moral: When working for this legally minded supermodel, always *ask*. And then get it in writing.

4

THE CELEBRITY IMAGE—OR, MAKING YOURSELF INCREDIBLE EVEN IF YOU'RE JUST A JERK

CELEBRITIES SPEND A LOT of time and a lot of energy (and a lot of money) cultivating the right image and making sure the public sees only that image—the image, of course, of a sexy, kind, quasi-omnipotent god.

Naturally, underneath said image, the average celebrity is an asshat. As we shall see below . . .

Are Celebrities Egotists?

Do celebrities believe in their own press? Do they buy into the image they've presented to the world? These are pressing questions, ones that the great minds have grappled with. It takes a certain amount of confidence to be a performer, a healthy appreciation of oneself. But is that egotism? Are celebrities egotists? Hmm . . . Why don't we take a look at what some of them have said, and see if we can come up with an answer.*

*Yes.

"You look wonderful. God, you're handsome!"

    —actor WARREN BEATTY, overheard in a bathroom, looking at a mirror

"I don't care if people think I'm an overactor. People who think that would call Van Gogh an overpainter."

    —actor JIM CARREY

"I think of everything I do as history in the making."

    —SEAN (DIDDY) COMBS

"It sounds vain, but I could probably make a difference for almost everyone I ever met if I chose to involve myself with them either professionally or personally."

    —actor KEVIN COSTNER

"I think every decade has an iconic blonde—like Marilyn Monroe or Princess Diana—and right now, I'm that icon."

    —PARIS HILTON

"Any man in Hollywood will meet me if I want that. No, make that any man *anywhere.*"

    —actress SHARON STONE

"I hate tooting my own horn, but after Steven [Spielberg] saw *Yentl,* he said, 'I wish I could tell you how to fix your picture, but I can't. It's the best film I've seen since *Citizen Kane.*' "

    —BARBRA STREISAND

"When I'm really hot, I can walk into a room and if a man doesn't look at me, he's probably gay."

    —actress KATHLEEN TURNER

IF YOU'RE PULLED OVER BY THE COPS, WHAT DO YOU SAY?

If you're a celebrity with a rather high opinion of yourself, you say:

"I'm a movie star. Can I talk to my entertainment lawyer?"
—ACTRESS NATASHA LYONNE, WHO STARRED IN *AMERICAN PIE,* TALKING
TO HER ARRESTING OFFICER IN FLORIDA'S MIAMI–DADE COUNTY.
LYONNE WAS ARRESTED ON CHARGES OF DRUNK AND CARELESS
DRIVING AND LEAVING THE SCENE OF AN ACCIDENT.

"I was late . . . and I got nominated for an Emmy. . . . Couldn't
I please go?"
—ACTRESS KRISTIN DAVIS, WHO RECEIVED A TICKET FOR HAVING OVERLY
DARK WINDOWS ON HER CAR. (THE POLICE ANSWERED, "NO.")

(If you're Mel Gibson, you may wish to add comments on the religious affiliation of the officers [see page 12] or ask female officers, "What do you think *you're* looking at, sugar tits?"

A Picture Paints a Thousand Words—and All of Them Are "Ego"

Speaking of healthy egos . . .

EGOTIST	"I LOVE ME" ITEM	COMMENTS
Usher	$1 million watch with his face on the face	Designed by Damon Dash; also has 1,106 diamonds on it . . . and was displayed, for some reason, at the Natural History Museum in London
Shaquille O'Neal	Alleged life-size statue of self outside of Miami mansion	Stands near dock
Seal and Heidi Klum	Large nude photos of them with their kids, hanging on the walls of their home	According to the New York *Daily News*'s Gatecrasher, the photos "leave no doubt what [Heidi] sees in Seal."
Mariah Carey	Life-size cake depicting herself	Carey ordered the cake for the 35th b-day party she threw herself; the 5'9" cake was prepared by 17 bakers, cost $9,500, and was a sponge cake filled with praline butter.
Star Jones	Gold-framed shot of self in bathroom	Visible in photos on a Realtor's website when Star had put her NYC penthouse triplex up for sale. The photo appeared to be a publicity head shot. We are not sure why she felt it was a nice touch in the bathroom. Perhaps she likes looking at herself for inspiration while relieving herself?

Brown-nosing for Big Bucks: How Celebrities Pander to Create the "Right" Image

Pandering celebrities suck up to their audience or fans the way . . . well, the way they (maybe) sucked up to, or sucked *something of*, their producers, many years before when they were beginning their careers. No, forget that. . . . It's just a vicious rumor.

But pandering is an art form that many celebrities are *experts* at. In their oh-so-deft ways they subtly let their fans know what wonderful nonracist, nonsexist people they are. The key is *subtlety*—the star doesn't announce the fact that he, for example, loves Jews, he just cleverly slips in the pertinent fact after waxing rhapsodic about something else. We decided to get rid of the subtle part and reveal how wonderful these stars are, and say it straight out. Why pander when you can say it out loud?

Sharon Stone Employs JEWS! And She's PROUD of It!

Sharon revealed her amazing pro-Semitism during a rather long-winded interview with Jon Stewart on *The Daily Show,* in which she talked about her trip to Israel and how she kissed someone for Middle Eastern peace:

> "People just are sitting there going, like, 'I don't care what she's saying, I don't care what she's saying, I just want to know, does she get naked in the movie? Is she naked? Nude nude nude naked? Do I see her boobies? I don't care what she's saying, I don't care, I don't care, is she naked?' So let's just get through to that . . . YES! [. . .]And I called my publicist, who's this great, Jewish woman . . ."

Actress Margaret Avery Is a Po' Humble Li'l God-Fearin' Country Girl Who Deserves an Oscar So *Bad,* Lawd, for *The Color Purple*

Instead of relying on her talent, or lack of it, and luck, or lack of it, actress Margaret Avery, up for an Oscar as Best Supporting Actress for the film *The Color Purple,* wrote a letter to Academy voters that explained precisely why she deserved to win. Importantly, she thanked God, which showed just how truly humble and deserving she was. She had the letters published in the Hollywood trade papers:

> "Well God, I guess the time has come fo' the Academy voters to decide whether I is one of the Best Supporting Actresses this year or not! Either way, thank you Lord, for the opportunity. Your little daughter, Margaret."

Madonna Is *So* Not Condescending! She *Likes* and *Understands* Workers

Madonna, the super-rich singer of humble origins who now seems to be pretending she's of the English country gentry, complete with British accent, tweeds, dogs, and Kabbalah . . . no wait a minute. . . . Anyway, before her English phase, she liked to emphasize how she was "just a middle-class girl from Michigan. It [extravagance] is just not in me." She liked to talk about the tough times before fame:

> "I had to clean houses—it was gross. I had to clean the toilet bowls of boys I went to school with. No, there's nothing more degrading than being someone's housekeeper. I mean, God bless my housekeeper and . . . well . . . all my housekeepers!"

We agree, God bless 'em all, each and every house-keeper. Even if they do disgusting, degrading jobs.

"I Am Just So Effing Cool": Creating That Cool Celebrity Image

Some celebrities know that cool is where it's at, man. They try to cultivate a certain je ne sais quoi that is supposed to prove that they're beyond hip, beyond phat, beyond what-ever the word-du-jour is.

Sometimes they kind of overdo it. . . .

But no matter. Cool is here to stay. And, in fact, with the wonderful diversity of our country, there are now many wonderful *different* kinds of celebrity cool.

Cool Type #1: The "'50s-Style, You Dig?" Cool Celebrity Personality

How to Be This Type of Cool: Be handsome, well-groomed, play poker well—and drink. Very heavily. Overuse certain words. (We won't tell you which.)

Best Example: Actor Peter Lawford, a member of Hol-lywood's so-called Rat Pack of hip stars, including Frank Sinatra

> "This French dame—this French reporter—comes up to me and says, 'Êtes-vous un Rat?' She's asking me, am I a Rat? I don't dig. Then I dig. She's asking me about the Rat Pack, you dig? But there's not a word in French for Rat Pack, you dig?"

Cool Type #2: The "Yo, Nigga, I'm a Thugged Whaat Man Who All de Niggas Say Is a Like a Badass Nigga" Cool Celebrity Personality

How to Be This Type of Cool: Listen to Diddy and other rappers and make believe you're a badass kind yourself. Practice in front of the mirror after your shower. Use terms like "thugged." Work on pronunciation—e.g., "a" instead of "er." Speak in short sentences. You may want to define your terms to the incognoscenti. Caution: Do not try this out in a real ghetto or with real rappers.

Best Example: Caucasian actor Mark Wahlberg, here speaking about Bill Clinton:

> "Bill is thugged out, you know. Bill's OG—original gangsta. . . . You've got to give him his props."

(Notice Mark's helpful definition of "OG"; quite obviously, he expects his fellow white listeners to be unsure of exactly what he's saying.)

Cool Type #3: The "I'm from the 2000s but I'm So Cool and Laid Back Just Like the '60s Even Though I Wasn't Born Yet but I Did See *Woodstock* on TV So I Know" Cool Celebrity Personality

How to Be This Type of Cool: Watch *The Last Waltz,* or *Woodstock.* Grow longish hair, meditate, learn yoga, smoke a lot of weed. Think of everything as being one, hanging together, and pulsating or vibrating. Don't worry: If you smoke enough, it will happen or you won't know so it won't bother you. Or you might be a natural, like actor Matthew McConaughey.

Best Example: Matthew McConaughey

> "To get my resources, I have to hang. I have to know and be in touch with and keep the pulse of every walk of life, man."

Cool Type #4: The "I Am a Creative Genius" Cool Personality

How to Be This Type of Cool: Be bizarre. Use acid imagery. Drink blood.

Best Example: Actor Nicolas Cage

> "I am not a demon. I am a lizard, a shark, a heat-seeking panther. I want to be Bob Denver on acid playing the accordion."

When Bad Celebrities Need Good Publicists

Excuses, Excuses.

Most of us, caught doing something we shouldn't, have to make excuses. All on our own. But not celebrities. They've got the money to hire expert publicists, who can protect that ol' image and make any misdemeanor, sexual perversion, drug-induced coma, etc., etc., sound just *fi-ine*!

Or sort of fine.

Or kind of fine.

Or not so fine . . .

Tom Hanks Says Asian-American Rocker Looks Like Pedicab Driver

This is the equivalent of saying that an African American looks like one of those minstrel singers, i.e., it's not a good thing to do . . . but it happened. Hanks, while attending a party at New York's Tavern on the Green, reportedly told Alex Wong, the lead singer for the Animators, that he "looked like one of those pedicab drivers." Witnesses said Wong did not seem to find this a charming comment.

Expert PR Excuse: Tom's spokesperson clarified: "He only meant that he was impressed with his physique because he was so muscular and lean like the guys who drive pedicabs all day."

Ah, yes. But of course.

Paris Hilton Caught Parking in Handicapped Space

Paris Hilton, certainly not handicapped physically (the cerebral cortex doesn't count), was seen parking in a space reserved for handicapped drivers. Not just once. Residents of a pricey Los Angeles apartment complex complained that whenever Hilton visited boyfriend quarterback Matt Leinart, she utilized the telltale spots reserved for those not able to walk very well, you know, the spaces reserved for those with the wheelchair license plates or tags. There's usually a picture of the wheelchair, and blue lines for those who, like Paris, might have some trouble *reading*.

Expert PR Excuse: Hilton's spokesman Elliot Mintz cleverly confronted this alleged selfish behavior this way: "I find the reports surprising."

That definitely clears things up.

Russell Crowe Compares Sharon Stone to a Great Ape

Russell Crowe appeared to compare Sharon Stone, first to one species of great ape, specifically a chimpanzee; then to another species, specifically an orangutan.

To be more specific, in a discussion of cosmetic surgery Crowe appeared to suggest that Sharon Stone had gone under the knife (which one has to admit is highly plausible, unless the actress is different from anyone else on the planet for not having telltale facial sags and wrinkles at her age). Referring to Stone, Crowe said, "A lot seems to have changed," i.e., her face. He then added, "You can end up looking like a startled chimpanzee. The eyes are gone, the lips are like rubber tires—or more like an orangutan that has been kicked in the arse. (For the culturally deprived noncognoscenti, "arse" is British for "ass.")

Expert PR Excuse: A Crowe rep explained it succinctly: "It was completely taken out of context." Out of context?

Keith Richards Says Mick Jagger Has a Small Penis

Here's *exactly* what Keith said about Mick Jagger:

> "His cock's on the end of his nose. And a very small one at that. Big balls. Small cock."

This is a hard statement to get out of, even for Keith Richards's expert PR handlers. Let's look at what Keith said about Mick again.

> "His cock's on the end of his nose. And a very small one at that. Big balls. Small cock."

It seems indisputable to us that Keith Richards is saying that Mick Jagger has a very small penis, with the not very offsetting advantage of having rather large testicles. This is not a very popular thing to say about a friend or an acquaintance—it tends to make them enemies.

Expert PR Excuse: Here's where you need the best PR money can buy; getting out of this one is a toughie. Keith's spokesman handled it this way: He said,

> "Keith apologized to Mick because he was trying to be complimentary and ended appearing offensive."

Er, trying to be complimentary . . . ? We no get.

The spokesman elaborated further, adding, "He did say that Mick had big balls as in he admired him because he was gutsy and courageous. How would he know anything about the size of his willy?"

Er, but then why did he say it was small?

Richard Gere Disses Handicapped Boy and Girl Who Breathes with a Trachea Tube

This is one of those stories that sounds like it's straight out of Charles Dickens long before the requisite happy ending: 15-year-old Brian Glassmacher, who along with his 17-year-old sister, Kailyn, suffers from a rare form of muscular dystrophy, is deaf, and is confined to a wheelchair, approached the great Buddhist actor (and best friend of the Dalai Lama) at the White House Correspondents' Dinner in Washington, D.C., and asked him to pose for a snapshot.

"My sister"—who is also deaf and breathes with the aid of a trachea tube—the boy reported, "was also there, and she really loves all of his movies—even more than I do," Brian said. "She really wanted him to come to the table, but it was really disappointing."

"Maybe later," the 55-year-old Gere was quoted as saying. "I'm hard of hearing and I have a bad hip. We all have problems."

(Parenthetical insight: We do indeed, but most of us are spared trachea tubes.)

An hour later, the boy asked again, and again Gere refused. "May I please finish my dinner?"

Finally, when the dinner ended, and with Brian's wheelchair blocking his exit, Gere consented to a photograph with the handicapped boy and his sister.

Meanwhile, *other* celebrities, such as quarterback Donovan McNabb and Constantine Maroulis from *American Idol,* cheerfully posed and signed autographs for the two Glassmachers.

Expert PR Excuse: According to Gere's publicist, Alan Nierob, "I'm sure Richard conducted himself as he always does—in the most gracious and respectable manner." Tell that to the kid with the trachea tube, Dicky!

Russell Crowe Throws Telephones at Hotel Staff

Most of us on the planet remember this very widely reported incident in which the famous, sexy, fabulously handsome, and temperamental international film star of great talent and importance got angry at a minor human hotel concierge at the Mercer Hotel in SoHo, New York, and threw a telephone at the man. Crowe was arrested for what police viewed as a criminal, and very unreasonable, assault on another human being.

Expert PR Excuse: Outside of the police station, Crowe's attorney explained it all in a way that allowed us fans to understand the reasonableness of Crowe's actions. According to Gerald Lefcourt: "This arose because he was trying to get his wife on the phone in Australia. He was in his room. He couldn't get a line and there was a disagreement."

Question: What would you do in a disagreement? The answer is now obvious to us—throw the phone.

Sienna Miller Has Her Toes Sucked Publicly

It's one thing to behave inappropriately in public when you're a big star—it's another to behave like one *before* you're a *super* big star. This was the purported problem with Sienna Miller, a British star-about-to-get-really-big and former g-friend to Jude Law, who was apparently acting it up a little too much at *Vanity Fair*'s post-Oscar party in 2006. She was seen hiking up her dress, waving her legs in the air, and having her foot nibbled by actress Tara Summers.

According to one witness: "Everyone was talking about

how Sienna was totally over-the-top. These pictures have seriously damaged her reputation." According to a Hollywood producer: "It's one thing to be gossiped about, but it's quite another to have pictures of yourself in that kind of clinch plastered all over a magazine. Hollywood is notoriously straightlaced when it comes to the behavior of a young star. This is an industry town. Actresses who expect to be taken seriously simply don't get drunk and behave like this in public."

Expert PR Excuse: Even though there were photos and eyewitnesses, Sienna Miller's spokesperson explained it in the "It didn't happen mode," i.e., deny, deny, and deny some more. "They have just wrapped a film together and they were just sitting next to each other at a party. Nothing more than that. We've had no complaints."

Charlie Sheen Has Had Sex with 5,000 Women

Some people would be proud of this, but it doesn't make for a family-film-friendly Hollywood image. So when *Maxim* reported that Sheen had reportedly slept with 5,000 women, his PR flacks got to work.

Expert PR Excuse: A Sheen PR type tried to put it in a logical context, asking: "How does one keep count of these things?" Er, that's not the point, Charlie.

When Bad Celebrities Make Bad Excuses

Some celebrities are real do-it-yourselfers. When faced with accusations of inappropriate behavior, they go into their *own* spin mode.

The problem is, sometimes they're even worse than the professionals.

Celebrity: Model Christie Brinkley's husband, celebrity architect Peter Cook

The Dirty Deed: Had torrid affair with 18-year-old former toy-store clerk turned architect-assistant and would-be singer. Later it surfaced that this was not the first nubile young thing he had studied architecture with in the nude.

The Bad Excuse: "This is an aberration. I'm sorry. I'm contrite. I'm stupid. Foolish. No excuse. I love my wife. . . . For a lifetime I've tried to prove how much I love her."

Comment: You prove your love to your wife by sleeping with cute teenagers? Okay. Uh-huh. Real logical.

Celebrity: Courtney Love

The Dirty Deed: Failed to show up in court to answer charges relating to her arrest for "possession of a controlled substance," the controlled substance presumably being some sort of narcotic but we're just guessing.

The Bad Excuse: I didn't show up for court because I didn't have a professional bodyguard.

Comment: The rather bizarre nature of the excuse tends to support the hypothesis that the "controlled substances" were somewhat mind-warping and narcotic in nature.

Celebrity: Johnny Depp

The Dirty Deed: Trashed (and yes, we mean *trashed*) his hotel room. Reportedly he was having a fight with then-girlfriend Kate Moss.

The Bad Excuse, Version 1: The big *bug* excuse. "There was a bug in the place that I was trying to kill. This thing had tried to attack me and tried to suck my blood—a big cockroach. And I tried to get it, I tried to whack it. I'd miss and smash a lamp . . ."

The Bad Excuse, Version 2: The big *rat* excuse. "I can only say that I'm human and I was chasing a huge rat in the hotel room and I just kept swatting at it. I couldn't catch it, and it just jumped out the window."

Comment: A hint of Freudian displacement theory— i.e., Kate Moss as bug, or as rat—is suggested.

Celebrity: Actor Eddie Murphy

The Dirty Deed: Picked up transvestite hooker by road in West Hollywood at 4:45 in the morning.

The Bad Excuse: He was "helping her." "It's not the first hooker that I've helped out. I was being a Good Samaritan."

Comment: What a *selfless* and *caring* gentleman, cruising Hollywood streets in the early morning looking for hookers to rescue, when he could be inside his multimillion-dollar mansion instead, consorting with expensive call girls.

Celebrity: Kevin Federline, then-husband to singer Britney Spears—and aspiring rapper

The Dirty Deed: In a word, "PopoZao." This was the first rap single (or is "bomb" the better word?) that the so-far-not-so-amazingly-musically-talented K-Fed foisted on the as yet unready world.

The Bad Excuse: According to some reports, the deviously clever Mr. Britney stated that he actually *planned* the whole thing—he deliberately wrote and performed an absolutely terrible rap song: "That way, when I come out with my real shit, people are fucking blown away," he allegedly said.

Comment: The disastrous reception of his later performances makes us wonder if Federline is continuing to deliberately produce critical and popular bombs, just waiting for that (ever elusive) day when he really blows the world away with his talent. Minor nagging point: Call us cynical, but why was Kevin-boy sweating so much promoting "PopoZao" on MTV if he thought it was so bad? Or was this just yet *another* clever PR ploy by the nefariously clever aspiring-rapper genius?

Celebrity: Kathleen Turner

The Dirty Deed: Publicly admitted having a drinking problem.

The Bad Excuse: She was just *pretending*! She actually had rheumatoid arthritis!

Comment: The thickening allegedly alcohol-swilling actress explained that she feared that she wouldn't find work if it came out that she had rheumatoid arthritis because of Hollywood's obsession with youth, so instead—*she faked being an alcoholic!* This excuse sounds a teensy weensy bit dicey to us. First of all, rheumatoid arthritis isn't related to age at all—you can get it at any age. And then did Kathleen also fake the reported threat from her husband to divorce her if she didn't stop drinking, as well as fake checking into a $560-a-day clinic to stop her habit? If so, a very *impressive* acting job, indeed.

Celebrity: Winona Ryder

The Dirty Deed: Caught shoplifting by Saks Fifth Avenue security guard.

The Bad Excuse: "I was told that I should shoplift. My director said I should try it out."

Comment: Isn't this taking method acting a little too far?

Celebrity: Diana Ross

The Dirty Deed: Spotted driving erratically, pulled over by police and asked to stand on one leg and count to ten.

The Bad Excuse: Got lost trying to find video store. Incidentally, Ross was unable to comply with police requests—i.e., count to ten and stand on one foot. Instead she fell down and burst out laughing.

Comment: Police didn't join in the laughter; instead they charged her with drunk driving.

Celebrity: Actor Jerry Lewis

The Dirty Deed: Dissed women in general after getting a bad review from one woman: "You can't accept one individual's [opinion], particularly if it's a female and you know—God willing, I hope, for her sake it's not the case—but when they get a period, it's really difficult for them to function as normal human beings."

The Bad Excuse: As a highly sexed man, actually wasn't dissing them at all: "I was not attacking the female gender by any means—not with the type of sex drive I have, honey. I have nothing against women. As a matter of fact there's something about them I love, but I just can't put my finger on it."

Comment: To put it in Jerry Lewis vernacular, Hey, nice lady! Apology accepted?

Quién Es Más Macho?: Stars with Manly Images . . . and Not-So-Manly Proclivities

Stars—male ones, in particular, for some reason—often like to present a very *macho* image to the public. They want people to think of them as real belly-up-to-the-bar, ride-a-hog, super-manly kinda guys.

But some of these supposed manly men have some not-so-little . . . well, let's call them "quirks" that might detract a bit from their image if the public ever found out.

You know, like all those manly men who wear lingerie.

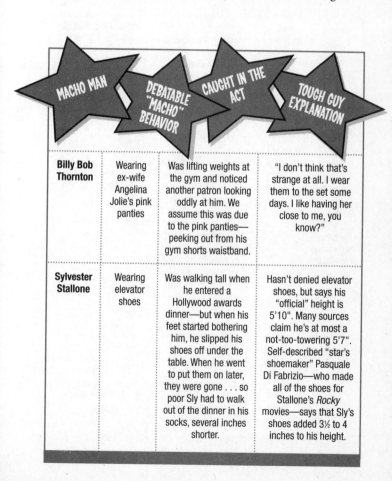

MACHO MAN	DEBATABLE "MACHO" BEHAVIOR	CAUGHT IN THE ACT	TOUGH GUY EXPLANATION
Billy Bob Thornton	Wearing ex-wife Angelina Jolie's pink panties	Was lifting weights at the gym and noticed another patron looking oddly at him. We assume this was due to the pink panties—peeking out from his gym shorts waistband.	"I don't think that's strange at all. I wear them to the set some days. I like having her close to me, you know?"
Sylvester Stallone	Wearing elevator shoes	Was walking tall when he entered a Hollywood awards dinner—but when his feet started bothering him, he slipped his shoes off under the table. When he went to put them on later, they were gone . . . so poor Sly had to walk out of the dinner in his socks, several inches shorter.	Hasn't denied elevator shoes, but says his "official" height is 5'10". Many sources claim he's at most a not-too-towering 5'7". Self-described "star's shoemaker" Pasquale Di Fabrizio—who made all of the shoes for Stallone's *Rocky* movies—says that Sly's shoes added 3½ to 4 inches to his height.

MACHO MAN	DEBATABLE "MACHO" BEHAVIOR	CAUGHT IN THE ACT	TOUGH GUY EXPLANATION
Nick Lachey	Used to like wearing then-wife's high heels	Those crazy newlyweds put a little spice in their love life (or so they said) by having Nick strut around the house in Jessica Simpson's heels. "It was sort of a kinky thing we liked to get into," he told *Elle* magazine.	This begs the question: Are his feet abnormally small or are hers abnormally large?
Justin Timberlake (okay, so we're stretching it, since he's not that macho to begin with . . .)	Needs help to kill spiders	Refused to enter the plush hotel room he was going to stay in because . . . there was (gasp) a SPIDER in there. Was forced, like any macho guy, to call the reception desk to ask for someone to come up and kill the tiny, but clearly threatening, arachnid.	"I'm really, really scared of spiders. I just hate them."
Justin Timberlake (again)	Sounds like a wuss when he talks	Was turned down for two major film roles and wondered why . . . then learned that the casting directors had rejected him because he sounded like a 12-year-old boy.	The proactive Timberlake has been taking voice lessons and is doing intensive voice exercises to sound less like Doogie Howser and more like a man.

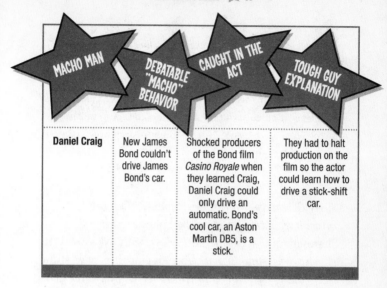

	MACHO MAN	DEBATABLE "MACHO" BEHAVIOR	CAUGHT IN THE ACT	TOUGH GUY EXPLANATION
Daniel Craig	New James Bond couldn't drive James Bond's car.	Shocked producers of the Bond film *Casino Royale* when they learned Craig, Daniel Craig could only drive an automatic. Bond's cool car, an Aston Martin DB5, is a stick.		They had to halt production on the film so the actor could learn how to drive a stick-shift car.

Celebrities' Warm and Fuzzy Relationship with the Image Makers of the Press

As Russell Crowe once said, "Everyone has a job to do. See, there are people who are in the arts . . . and there are parasites who sniff around other people's poo."

He is speaking, of course, of journalists.

Yes, some celebrities just aren't terribly *fond* of those ink-stained—or should we say carpal-tunnel/repetitive-injury-due-to-keyboards-prone—wretches. And those celebrities know how to show it.

Surly Celebrity Interviewee: Gérard Depardieu
Interview Style: Drunk, theological, abrupt

He forced a journalist to meet him 2½ hours early (or else no interview). As the lucky writer further explains:

He weaves in and plops down in the chair in front of me. He is pale and sweating, his eyes are rolling in his head, his face looks like Silly Putty. He is slurring-word drunk, but being Depardieu, his diction is perfect. He orders a half-bottle of wine for us. Throws it back like water. Talks for about 15 minutes about St. Augustine, the saint, not the town. Then he declares, "I have to go to sleep now," gets up and walks out.

Surly Celebrity Interviewee: Shannen Doherty
Interview Style: Defensive, bad phone manners

Shannen did a phone interview with *Newsweek* in which she was *supposed* to be plugging her new show called *Breaking Up with Shannen Doherty.* After three general questions (including a simple "How are you?"), the reporter logically asked Shannen about her own rather well-publicized breakups, including one in which she allegedly tried to run over her boyfriend. Shannen was not abmused.

SHANNEN: "I am not going to have things rehashed from 15 years ago. I'm not going to combat lies. I can already tell what's going to be in your article."
REPORTER: "But—"
SHANNEN: "Let me hang up and call my publicist and then we'll reconvene, because I'm not going down this path."
—*CLICK*

Shockingly, Doherty did not call the reporter back.

Surly Celebrity Interviewee: Gwyneth Paltrow
Interview Style: Stick-up-the-ass

In the words of one reporter quoted in the *New York Post*'s Page Six, she "just won't answer questions. She'll tell you stuff like, 'I don't like to talk to reporters,' and you are like, 'Well, then why are you here?' She won't tell you a thing and only wants to talk about her 'art' and has fake graciousness."

THE FLIP SIDE: AN AMAZINGLY OVERLY FRIENDLY CELEBRITY INTERVIEW STYLE, COURTESY OF BEN AFFLECK

Never let it be said that Ben is standoffish and cold. Here—in excerpts from a 2004 interview with Montreal TV personality Anne-Marie Losique—Ben exhibits a warm appreciation for the interviewer and her pert breasts:

"They would like it better if you did the show topless. . . . You usually show a lot more cleavage than this. What's the story, why are you covering it up today? . . . It's Sunday morning? That never stopped you before from getting the titties out. Who're you trying to fool, it's Sunday morning. You could be in church. You should have that rack on display. . . . You know you should work at Fox in L.A. You'd blend right in, they'd love you. Fox L.A. they have a pole that they dance on. . . . These breasts are very firm. Suspiciously firm I have to say. They are like two giant stones. . . . Should we do a Janet Jackson thing? Are you wearing your nipple ring?"

Surrealistic Interview Moments—or, We Definitely Hope They Were High at the Time. . . .

Some celebrities are a little more forthcoming with journalists but we're not sure what's coming forth.

They just seem a little . . . surrealistic.

Kate Bosworth Talks About Tea!

"God, I'm hot from that tea. Woo. All of the sudden, I'm like, woo, warm! That actually happens to me if I have a hot drink? Yeah, yeah."

Joaquin Phoenix Talks About Frogs! In His Hair!

"Do I have a large frog in my hair? Something's crawling out of my scalp . . . I feel it. I'm not worried about the looks. I'm worried about the sensation of my brain being eaten. . . . What did you ask me?"

Amanda Bynes Talks About Nice People Being Nice! (Except When They're Not!)

When asked about the public's reaction to her on the street: "That is really nice when they are nice. When they are not so nice, it's not nice."

Paris Hilton Talks About Whatever!

Excerpted from a *New York Post* interview about her role in *House of Wax:* "At first, I wasn't too keen on the idea, but, um, whatever."

Q: "Do you think people are mean to you?"
PARIS: "Yeah. But, whatever. I don't mind."
Q: "Why is everyone so mean?"
PARIS: "I don't know. I'm easy to do it to, I guess. But whatever . . ."

Q: "You don't think people resent you?"

PARIS: "Well, maybe someone's trying to be cool, and like, 'Ooh, look. I'm cool. I'm clapping.' But, whatever."

Ben Affleck Talks About Vomiting! (Metaphorically!)

When asked how it felt being out of the media's eye after his impending marriage to Jennifer Lopez went kaput: "It's the sort of vague calm you get after vomiting—where the vomit itself is rather unpleasant, but when it's over, it brings a kind of strange peace."

NEWS FLASH! JENNIFER LOPEZ IS REALLY BORING!

According to an anonymous reporter quoted by the *New York Post*'s Page Six, J Lo is "dull. She is so boring. She arrived an hour late and said her favorite book was something like *Meditations for Women Who Do Too Much*. She doesn't read, she doesn't watch TV or movies— nothing."

Things We'd Rather Not Know About Celebrities: The Too Much Information Awards

Speaking about vomit . . . In their quest to let their adoring publics adore them even further, celebrities like to share snippets of their personal lives. Sometimes these snippets are the equivalent of fungus-infected toenail clippings— i.e., things we'd just as soon not ponder.

Herewith, then, the TMI Awards, given to those celebrities who feel the need to unburden themselves to such a degree that we the public get more than a little grossed out.

The "We Don't Give a Shit About Your Shit" Award goes to . . . the cast of *Will and Grace*

Who, appearing on *Oprah* to talk about how it felt that their long-running show was ending, er, unloaded about some behind-the-scenes action:

SEAN HAYES: "Before each show I have a PSP. Not a Sony PlayStation. I have a pre-show poop. Because I get a nervous stomach."

DEBRA MESSING: "And we cannot start the show until he has had his poop. So we check in."

MEGAN MULLALLY: "We had to wait a couple of times . . ."

OPRAH: "Everybody's laughing, but isn't a poop so freeing?"

The "Diarrhea of the Mouth" Award goes to . . . Jenny McCarthy

Who shared a very special moment she had at a *Playboy* signing:

"I once had really bad diarrhea at a *Playboy* autograph signing. I was squeezed into a tight red dress, dripping in sweat, and knew something was not right. But blond model's heroic attempts to ignore it were sadly in vain. I just kept having my picture taken with the fans. But then I was like: 'Oh no, the demon is about to be unleashed.' And it was unleashed for about 20 guys to witness. I knew at that point in my career all I was supposed to do was turn men on, but just ended up grossing them out."

The "No, We're Not Dying to Hear About Your Diet" Award goes to . . . Kate Winslet

Who felt the need to explain how well her new vegetarian diet was working:

"I'm holding so much water now I have a backside that looks like a cauliflower. And other parts of my body resemble strange vegetables like squashes or things like that."

The "Fun Funeral Snacks" Award goes to . . . Larry Hagman

Who explained exactly what he wants done to his body after dying:

"Cremation's fine, but it uses an awful lot of energy. Burying someone in a steel casket doesn't do any good. I want to return to the earth as soon as possible."

So what does he want done?

"When I die, I want my friends to eat me. I want to be fed through a wood chipper, be spread over a wheat field, then have a cake baked from the crop for all my pals to munch on."

(He also wants pot put in that cake.)

The "People Whose Showers We'll Never Use" Award goes to . . . Madonna

Who, during an appearance on *The Late Show with David Letterman,* told David (and the viewing audience) that she was a fan of peeing in the shower to help kill fungal organisms.

And the big winner of them all, the winner of the grand TMI, the "WAAAYY Too Much Information" Award goes to . . .
Bobby Brown

Who, on his reality TV show *Being Bobby,* allowed the cameras to record this lovely moment between him and then-wife Whitney Houston:

> "I've had to dig a dootie bubble out of your butt. . . . That turd was too big!"

Charmed, we're sure.

CELEBRITY ENEMA SUBSECTION

Readers interested in celebrity enemas will be pleased to know that singer Kim Wilde enjoyed hers very much, thank you:

> "My self-administered enema demystified me; that's why I did it. There was something very liberating about it."

CELEBRITIES AND THEIR WORK

LET US TURN NOW to the meat-and-potatoes side of celebrity: work. Or, in some cases, quasi-work.

How do celebrities go about their jobs? How do they manage to cope with all the work-related pressures? How do they make it look so easy?

We don't have the answers, but we do have some stupid examples of celebrities at work.

The Tough Life

It's easy to sneer at celebrities. But aren't we forgetting something important? *Celebrities don't have it easy.*

Okay, sure, they're pulling in millions of dollars for what seems to be minimal work, getting *more* millions for just showing up at events or publicizing some brand of something, getting freebies even though they can afford to pay for everything and anything while we poor slobs have to work our fingers to the bone, and they bop all over the place in first class unlike the rest of us sweating it out in ECONOMY CLASS, AND THEN THEY GET FREE TICK-

ETS, NOT TO MENTION THE FACT THAT THEY GET TO GO TO THEIR FRIENDS' PRIVATE *ISLANDS* WHILE WE'RE STUCK IN TRAFFIC TRYING TO GET TO THE FREAKING BEACH FOR CHRISSAKE . . .

Pardon us.

As we were saying, aren't we being unfair? Let us be democratic and open-minded here, then. Let us purge pettiness from our systems and admit that celebrities have it *tough*. Let us give credit where credit is due and truly *appreciate* the rigors of celebrity life.

Celebrities have difficult jobs.

Take Vanna White—the *Wheel of Fortune* letter turner, the perennially preserved plasticine-like "person" who reportedly makes from $3 to $5 million a year for her intensive game show work as well as other ventures: "It's not as easy as it looks, being on all the time. I mean, what happens if I'm in a bad mood?"

Or singer Barbra Streisand, who must actually perform for her living by singing for a few hours onstage! And on TV! As she put it: "Do you know what it's like to have to walk around in high heels and sing 35 songs a night, to have to diet to get into those dresses?" (Actually, we don't know. But it sounds so GRUELING! No wonder Babs is forced to retire every other year or so.)

Celebrities are STUCK doing their very difficult jobs.

For example, Keira Knightley is absolutely *miserable* being an actress who earns multimillions. She hates dealing with the press; she won't deal with print media (in her words: "I don't read any magazines or newspapers anymore because I find it really scary"); and she hates photographers. "I get really scared when I'm followed by photographers. I have, on many occasions, broken down in tears be-cause I find it terrifying."

Why not quit, you might think? (We thought it.) Well, the poor thing has no choice, you see. She has to suck it up and keep on being a famous actress, since she just doesn't have any other options. "I dropped out of school when I was 16 so there's nothing else I can do."

Celebrities have had to pay the price for their success.

Yeah, there's the loss of privacy thing, of course. But there are so many *other* things that celebrities have had to give up, things we selfish "norms" take for granted. Singer Beyoncé knows the high cost of fame, for example: "We were young and sacrificed a lot. I had to give up cheerlead-ing, as did the others."

Celebrities need great inner strength to cope with unimaginable stress arising from incidents that would never happen to plain ol' non-celebs.

Actress Gwyneth Paltrow describes a moment of ex-treme food-related bravery, Hollywood-style. She was star-ring with Matt Damon in *The Talented Mr. Ripley.* And poor Matt had to get thin. The scene they were shooting took three days—and Matt was aiming for his lowest weight. "At the end of the second day he had a pizza stand-ing by so he could eat. But we didn't finish the scene. It was so sad and he couldn't eat the whole thing the next night. That's bravery."

You can't even begin to imagine the gut-wrenching decisions they have to face.

Unique and disturbing decisions, at that. The kind that mere mortals can't begin to understand. Actress/model/

"designer" (Of beachwear. Theoretically.) Elizabeth Hurley shares her difficult dilemma: "If I had a [wedding] dress designed for me I'd be in absolute agony." Yup, poor Liz is buddies with too many top-notch designers. "I wouldn't know who to go to. I have so many friends in the fashion business, and I work with so many fabulous people, I'd be in absolute hell. I might just get married in an Elizabeth Hurley Beach kaftan." (Note: She gets extra points for plugging her fashion line.)

And they face even bigger money woes than we do.

Back in 2000, when there was a huge battle about Napster offering free music downloads, Madonna was extremely concerned. If Napster wasn't prevented from doing business, "people won't buy my records, and how will I pay for my daughter's schooling?" (Not to worry, though. Not only are free downloads no longer as prevalent, Madonna also was able to buy a $15 million home in London at the same time she was panicking about Lourdes's education.)

They have to live with the fact that they've incommoded others.

Paris Hilton feels the pain of others. But she also has had to develop a thick skin so as not to be ripped by remorse any time something negative happens as a result of her actions. "One time I arrived at a party in a helicopter. I kind of felt bad, because the wind from the propellers blew Champagne glasses out of people's hands. But I thought it was cool."

They're underappreciated.

Here celebrities give their *all* to make the world a happier place. But do they get enough thanks from their bosses? Hell no. Scarlett Johansson remembers a time when things were different. "Robert Redford gave me a silver bracelet, which I cherished. And I haven't gotten anything lately that was like that. The studio will send you a wilting fruit basket or some mediocre Champagne or maybe the newest iPod."

To add insult to injury, she notes that "some people get cars—that would be nice, but will they also pay for my parking?"

Possibly the worst thing of all: Celebrities make too much money. (Oh, the humanity . . .)

Country star Shania Twain knows what true pain is. True pain is making over $50 million in concert ticket sales in one year (not to mention all the bucks from record contracts). She'd so much rather be poor, she explained in an interview. "Money is a burden. All anybody needs is enough to eat and have a roof over their heads. Any more than that is a stress. My son is going to have money, and he's going to be stressed."

Interestingly, as of this writing, Twain still has not given away the bulk of her personal fortune. No, she's suffering with her money. Now that's one tough cookie!

Diva Demands: A Head-to-(Inflated)-Head Comparison

Speaking of the tough life, some stars get a raw deal. They're termed "divas" merely because they make teeny tiny requests—simple things, really—that they feel they're entitled to while they're working their poor fingers to the bone. Yet, for some reason, people construe these simple, teeny tiny demands as proof positive of divadom. We can't understand it.

The Diva: Demi Moore
The Teeny Tiny Demand: Transportation from work to a PTA meeting

Oh, yeah—the PTA meeting was in Idaho, and the studio was in Burbank, so the studio wound up shelling out $4,500 to pay for the attentive mom's private jet. (What? You thought she'd fly *commercial*?!?)

The Diva: Demi Moore (again)
The Teeny Tiny Demand: Plane to fly her from her Idaho home to New York City

Actually, it ended up being two planes. . . . When the first private plane came to pick her up, Demi noticed it was a tad too small—and she would have to (gasp) STACK HER LUGGAGE! Needless to say, this was untenable. She contacted her studio, Sony, and insisted on a second plane—so her baggage could fly to the East Coast unstacked.

The Diva: Diana Ross
The Teeny Tiny Demand: Wouldn't perform until marquee at Caesars Palace, Las Vegas, had her name only on it

Miss Ross is very persnickety about this, so her contract had language in it to that effect. Imagine her *shock*, then, when, on the day of the show, Ross found that the marquee did say DIANA ROSS in big letters, but also had SHEENA EASTON APPEARING IN TWO WEEKS in little letters . . . at the very bottom. Naturally, she refused to perform until the sign was changed—even though fans were already thronging into the venue. And, naturally, when the casino management assured her that the sign was fixed, she had to see for herself. She walked out of her dressing room, through the casino, and straight out the front doors to take a gander at the sign herself. Luckily, the managers hadn't lied—so she performed her show. But poor Diana felt woefully misunderstood: "Just because I have my standards, they think I'm a bitch," she commented.

The Diva: Unnamed star of *X-Men 2*
The Teeny Tiny Demand: Coffee chain barista on set

Hugh Jackman—one of the stars of *X-Men 2*—dubbed this one of the most preposterous examples of diva behavior he had ever seen. In his words: "The strangest thing I ever saw was while filming *X-Men 2*—I can't tell you the name, but one of the cast loves a particular coffee chain. This person liked an ice-blended drink, so a specialist was flown up and stayed on set for this person to have one cup a day. I used to talk to the guy because I felt sorry for him. He had to stand around all day and make one drink. I was like, 'You are fucking kidding me.' "

The Diva: Kim Basinger
The Teeny Tiny Demand: Producer-supplied cases of Evian water on set

There was one little catch: The Evian wasn't for drinking. It was needed to wash her hair.

The Diva: Julia Roberts
The Teeny Tiny Demand: Private jets and mansions for cast and crew of *Ocean's Twelve* while scenes were reshot

Scenes needed to be reshot; Julia insisted that the cast and crew be flown to Chicago by private jets and housed in three private mansions close by. No biggie. But the only reason the scenes needed to be reshot was that Julia wasn't crazy about the outfits she was wearing in them—and wanted them shot with her wearing clothes she liked more.

The Diva: Joan Crawford

The Teeny Tiny Demand: Wouldn't show up at publicity photo shoot because there was no limo to pick her up

As a star of the highest magnitude, Joan Crawford expected a limo (complete with chauffeur in uniform and a maid) to take her everywhere on the MGM lot. But one day, horror of horrors, the limo wasn't there to take her to a photo shoot. Needless to say, Ms. Crawford canceled the shoot. As she explained, "It's in my contract that I have a limousine." Okay, okay, this sounds reasonable, you may be thinking. Did we mention that the photo studio was only a few yards from Joan's dressing room?

The Diva: Jennifer Connelly

The Teeny Tiny Demand: Car and driver to chauffeur her to and from the set

Connelly—who interestingly has the same initials as Joan Crawford—was merely acting in the time-honored tradition when she took advantage of a chauffeured Cadillac Escalade to take her from the trailer in which she was staying to the set of *The Hulk*. And she was following in Crawford's footsteps—or, rather, tire tracks—in another way: Her trailer was only two blocks away from where they were shooting.

The Diva: Keira Knightley

The Teeny Tiny Demand: Alterations and lunch

Keira was doing the usual star thing and shopping for a gown at the designer's studio. She tried on a gown, asked for it to be altered (on the spot, natch), and then asked for lunch. After she ate—and after the gown had been altered—wouldn't you know it? She decided she didn't want the dress after all.

The Diva: Tommy Lee Jones
The Teeny Tiny Demand: No T-shirts. And NO WIRE HANG— Oops, we mean, NO LABELS!

Tommy Lee was promoting *Men in Black II*—and was scheduled for a photo shoot and interview at the City Club hotel in Manhattan. A source told the *New York Post* that there were several "musts" that had to be followed before he'd go ahead with the publicity effort. Must number one: His publicist went into the room ahead of him and announced, "Get rid of all T-shirts—if he even sees one, he'll walk off set." Once the offending shirts were removed, must number two came into play: The photo stylists had to cut the labels out of all the clothing he was going to wear in the shoot. But, naturally, there was a very good reason for this. The source explained, "Labels freak him out."

The Diva: Janet Jackson
The Teeny Tiny Demand: Properly chilled—and temperature-tested—water

When Janet Jackson was on the Johnny Vaughan show on Capital Radio in London, she asked for chilled Fiji spring water. And—to make sure it was the optimal temperature—she had a staff member slip a thermometer into it to be sure it was cold enough. (You will be glad to know that it was. We are sure she enjoyed the refreshing drink.)

The Diva: Demi Moore

The Teeny Tiny Demand: Needed a scene reshot in her film *The Scarlet Letter*

It cost the producers $50,000 when Demi decided a scene just *had* to be reshot—because her hair looked bad. (We assume this was for literary accuracy since Hester Prynne was known for her perfectly coiffed hair, wasn't she? Granted, we haven't read *The Scarlet Letter* since high school. . . .)

The Diva: Russell Crowe

The Teeny Tiny Demand: Studio payment for entourage member to be flown in and housed on production dollar during filming of *Master and Commander: The Far Side of the World*—costing the studio an extra $150,000

Crowe wanted Belinda Jeffrey there, dammit, and he was going to make sure the studio paid for it. Jeffrey was crucial to his performance! The studio, of course, paid. Oh, wait . . . did we mention that she was his fave hairdresser? (His hair looked AMAZING in the film, didn't it?)

The Diva: Jessica Simpson

The Teeny Tiny Demand: 40% of total available hotel rooms—plus $20 thou for hair and makeup, $80 thou for a production budget and more—all for appearing at an afterparty for the Video Music Awards

Clearly Jessica wanted this to be one helluva party. *People* magazine was sponsoring it at the exclusive Miami hotel the Setai. And Jess wanted things to be perfect. So she asked for a lot of money—and for over 30 hotel rooms for her entourage. Considering there were only 75 rooms at the hotel in total, this was a little dicey. *People* wound up saying the hell with it and pulling out as a sponsor.

The Diva: Jennifer Lopez

The Teeny Tiny Demand: Extra security at the Royal Variety Show in London

Problem was, J Lo reportedly wanted more security than even the queen was getting. The London police—following in the footsteps of Queen Victoria—were not amused, and didn't comply with her request.

The Diva: Gina Gershon (with weird fake Italian accent)

The Teeny Tiny Demand: $650 pair of shoes as a freebie

The shoes made Gershon stop production of the pilot for TV series *Ugly Betty.* She was playing a fashion diva à la Donatella Versace and had some killer shoes as part of her costume. When the producers wanted her to sign her contract sans lawyer, Gershon—in the quasi-Italian accent she was using for the role—argued with them and said not only would she not sign the contract until her lawyer read it, but also she just *had* to get the shoes. Gratis, of course. Later, her manager said: "Once she was connected with her rep, everything was cleared up in three minutes. There was no diva behavior, and they had a great day of shooting, and she loved playing the character. It sounds like someone is turning a comedic moment into drama."

Also-Ran Diva Demands—Which Just Didn't *Quite* Reach the Heights

The following need to work their attitude a bit more, as they folded in the face of dissension to their demands:

- **Mike Myers,** who, in the midst of filming *Wayne's World,* almost quit the film when he learned there was no margarine for his bagel. (He did, however, reconsider and decided to stay in spite in the margarine-less set.)

- **Paris Hilton,** who threatened to pull out of the Brit Awards until she got a Jacuzzi in her dressing room. (She did, however, decide to do the show after advisers pointed out that the $235,000 should make up for the lack of pulsating water jets.)

- **Martha Stewart,** who—prior to being charged with insider trading—said she'd leave her broker, Peter Bacanovic, and her brokerage, Merrill Lynch, unless they changed the hold music on the telephone. The music wasn't changed—but that could have been because the whole crew got called up on insider trading charges before it could be done.

SHARON STONE: PERKS "R" US

Sharon Stone doesn't play around. When she wants something, she wants it, dammit—and the riders (five pages' worth) she has gotten attached to her contracts prove it. (We are not sure, however, that she will continue to get such requests filled by producers—after the large egg *Basic Instinct 2* laid at the box office. She got paid $14 million. The film made $5.8 million in the United States.)

A few examples of what she "needed" to film *Basic Instinct 2*:

- Pilates equipment

- $3,500 per day for armed bodyguards

- no cigar smoking on set

- no oil-based smoke used for special effects

- chauffeured car with nonsmoking driver (must be approved by Stone)

- convertible sedan for personal use

- three nannies (at $1,500 per week)

- two assistants

- the right to approve of all catering (if not approved, personal chef)

- personal trainer

- cell phones and pagers

- lodging must be in presidential suite with two bedrooms

- first-class plane travel for six (should private jet not be available)

- deluxe motor home with a/c, heating, bed, private bathroom, shower, TV, VCR, refrigerator, telephone, stove, couch, stereo, and cellular fax machine ("no one receives better facilities," her rider states)

- all jewelry and wardrobe pieces worn during filming

The Celebrity Entourage: *Essential* Helpers for the True Celeb

To do a celebrity job properly, one needs minions. *Many* minions. An *entourage* of minions and hangers-on able to do special things . . . like swim the swirling and polluted waters of New York's East River to bring Sean Penn a much-needed cigarette.

You see, for an A-list celebrity (or any celebrity aspiring to such exalted status) having a plain old entourage is not enough. Anyone with a spare million can have one of those. The key is to have a *specialized* entourage; one in which each individual tagging along after the star has a specific, asinine, and essentially inane job function.

SPECIALIZED ENTOURAGE JOB TITLE	CELEBRITY EMPLOYER	JOB DESCRIPTION
Battery Putter-Inner	Rapper **Ludacris**	Change batteries. (Or take them out. Or put them in.) When one member of the hip-hop star's large entourage was asked what he did, he replied, "I do the batteries," and added that he was *particularly* responsible for the Game Boy batteries. (Talk about your specialization!)
Nipple Squeezer	Singer **Pink**	Just what the job title suggests. As Pink explains: "I need my nipples squeezed before every show. It gets me pumped to go onstage. My assistant Jackie has it down to a fine art."
Nipple Squeezer AND Icer	**Jennifer Lopez**	A two-person job. (One per breast? Or one for icing and the other for squeezing?) Squeezer/Icers were employed during the video shoot for "Jenny from the Block" to make certain nipples were erect and protruded through string vest "in just the right way."

SPECIALIZED ENTOURAGE JOB TITLE	CELEBRITY EMPLOYER	JOB DESCRIPTION
Darkening Team	Singer **Rod Stewart**	A specialized team who go to the hotel before Rod Stewart arrives and seal all cracks of light in the bedroom, since the star "cannot tolerate any light in the room for his afternoon nap."
Skirt-from-Touching-Floor Specialist	**Mariah Carey**	Self-explanatory. The diva employs a "petite Colombian woman" to keep her long skirts from touching the floor. Mariah also uses this woman for other specialized jobs, including carrying a Louis Vuitton backpack with bottled water.
Towel Hand-off Person	**Mariah Carey**	Hand the sometimes sweaty diva her towels.
Drink Holding/Lifting Specialist	**Mariah Carey**	Hold, then lift drink with straw to thirsty Mariah's lips. While Carey was signing copies of her album *The Emancipation of Mimi*, an assistant was right next to her with a cup, periodically lifting it to the busy diva's lips.

SPECIALIZED ENTOURAGE JOB TITLE	CELEBRITY EMPLOYER	JOB DESCRIPTION
Jewelry Jockey	**Nelly**	In charge of all the gold, silver, and crystal rocks Nelly is forced to travel with.
Towel Swinger	Rapper **N.O.R.E.**	Stand on stage and swing a towel around.
Umbrella Carrier	**Kim Basinger**	Sunny-day-only position. Basinger requires an assistant on sunny days whose job it is to carry an umbrella to ward off damaging sun rays.

"Is My Career About to Go Down the Toilet?": Omens of Career Meltdowns

When a celebrity's career—or "quasi-career" as befits cases such as the multi-untalented Paris Hilton—begins to go down the toilet, there are warning signals before the phones stop ringing and your agent dumps you.

Here are a few signs that maybe, just maybe, that career toilet is about to be flushed.

Courtney Can't Sell Her Own Coffin On eBay

EBay, the international online marketplace, is a great place to check on a star's popularity. Who's hot sells. And who's not doesn't. So what do we say when a half-crazed and fully annoying rock-etress named Courtney Love failed to get a good price for her Plexiglas grave casket on eBay? Bids reportedly topped out at a very paltry $560. (A bargain for casket shoppers, incidentally—except the shipping costs were probably *murderous*. Sorry.)

Poll Finds That People Would Rather Sleep with Saddam Hussein Than with Tom Cruise

This is relatively bad, to have Americans prefer a hated dictator of mass destruction to you. Or maybe it's just that big mustaches are in again.

Whatever, in a recent poll in *Stuff Magazine,* more people named Tom Cruise than named Saddam Hussein as the person they'd least like to share a camping tent with.

At least it was *close:* 41 percent said Tom was their worst choice, a close near tie with 39 percent picking Saddam.

Eminem's Uncle Can't Sell Eminem's Lyrics and Drawings on eBay

John Lennon's *scribbles* sell for the price of a small detached two-bedroom/two-bath house—but Eminem's uncle couldn't get the market to move past the price of a candy bar for a collection of the rapper's drawings, placed on eBay. They just didn't move.

According to Uncle Eminem: "After what happened . . . I decided to keep the items in the family and pass them down to the kids. [They] will only get more valuable as the years go by."

As online gossip column Tab Fab fabulously noted: "They would *have* to be worth more later, because what's less than zero?"

Paris Hilton's Single Hits the Charts, and Bounces— Down, Down, Down

In 2006, Paris's first CD sold a very lackadaisical 75,000 copies in the United States—compared with Christina Aguilera's first-week sales of 320,000. Her second-week sales were a paltry 30,000 or so. Hilton's rep, Elliot Mintz, said, "To me, [the album] sounds huge. For a newcomer, this is incredibly impressive."

Paris Hilton, a newcomer? Come on, Mintz. You can do better than that.

Speaking of Paris, Bouncers Don't Let Her into New York Hot Spots

The best way to learn that you're not hot is to hear it from a bouncer who is blocking your way into a happening place. That's what happened to Paris Hilton when she tried to get into the ultraselective NYC club Bungalow 8. She was told she couldn't get in because it was "full to capacity." According to a witness, poor Paris "was sobbing and kept saying she was Paris Hilton and she didn't understand."

Six days later, she tried to get into the Gramercy Park Hotel's Rose Bar to join celebs like Orlando Bloom, Winona Ryder, and Josh Lucas. The bouncer wouldn't let her in because of owner Ian Schrager's rule that "the likes of Paris Hilton and her ilk are not welcome here."

Is there a pattern here?

Alternative Careers for Celebrities

What if acting or singing isn't enough? Some celebrities want *more* out of life, like new careers.

And why not? After all, they're about as talented as they

come—they're celebrities! Many people believe they can do anything, and many celebrities seem to agree. Here, then, are some multitalented individuals who are challenging themselves—and offering unexpected new talents and skills to the world.

Keira Knightley

Old Career: Actress
New Career: Bricklaying
Reason: Possible global thermonuclear war

The sprightly young actress, who earns about $3 million per movie, plans to learn this trade—just in case. "Everyone laughs when I say I'm looking into bricklaying. But I decided if an apocalypse ever comes I'd like to be a skilled laborer and not be left behind at a campfire making gruel. My friend's looking for a job and we found out you can get £15 to £30 an hour for bricklaying. I've found the courses and the moment I have some spare time I want to do it. I'm sure I can find a positive experience in laying bricks."

Britney Spears

Old Career: Pop singer
New Career: Forensic scientist
Reason: TV show

According to a source quoted in Britain's *Daily Mirror* newspaper, the deductively minded Britney was inspired by TV's *extremely* realistic *Crime Scene Investigation*, which shows cool good-looking scientists cleverly solving all sorts of murders and other crimes in less than one hour. Another reason forensics was appealing: too much publicity and attention as a singer. A cool, isolated forensics lab without reporters seems more alluring. She even talked with Natalie Portman, who attended Harvard, about school life. Her then-husband Kevin Federline, no intellectual slouch himself, reportedly backed her decision.

Lance Bass

Old Career: Singer

New Career: Space scientist

Reason: Deep desire to do experiments in space

To accomplish this, Bass signed an initial deal with the Russian Aviation and Space Agency to rocket to the International Space Station. According to 'N Sync bandmate Joey Fatone, "People are always going, 'Oh, he's just going to go up in space and mess around and stuff.' But he actually wants to do a lot of different experiments. . . ." (As well as stand around going, "Look, I'm in space.") Unfortunately, the Russians don't view the scientist/rock star's work as particularly vital or important: "All he needs to know is how to put on his suit and what not to touch," one Russian official said. "We could even train a monkey to do this."

Jennifer Lopez

Old Career: Singer

New Career: President of the United States

Reason: Unknown, but possibly megalomania combined with a refined HGTV sensibility

Hey, whatever, she wants to serve the people of the United States as the first female president. She told a reporter, "The first thing I'd do is redecorate the White House—it doesn't look cozy." Is that presidential material or what?!

6

CELEBRITY PRODUCT LINES, ENDORSEMENTS, AND OTHER VERY IMPORTANT NON-CELEBRITY CELEBRITY BUSINESS VENTURES

CELEBRITIES ARE OFTEN NOT content making millions for acting and/or singing and/or spokesmodeling. And who can blame them? Why settle for mere millions when you can make *more* millions?

How? By delving into the world of non-celebrity celebrity business.

All those tough things like putting your name on perfume (and sometimes even having to smell it first!), accepting paychecks for having designers design things under your name, making appearances at special events for products that have your name on it. (Do you detect a theme here?)

Great Moments in Celebrity Business

Move over Sumner Redstone and all you Fortune 500 CEOs. The celebrities are here—and they have *ideas*!

**Creative Jennifer Lopez Sees a Need and Fills It:
Designer Jewelry for Deprived Dogs**

You may have noticed that most dogs are deprived in
the way of jewelry—but one far-sighted and big-butted
singer got off her cheeks and is doing something about it.
Jennifer Lopez is designing an entire range of jewelry for
canines. As an insider put it: "Jennifer just got creative and
wanted to extend the range of jewels for animals. She has
always found it somewhat frustrating that there are limited
accessories available for them."

Whether the star plans to extend her talents into the fe-
line or piscine pet areas was not reported.

**Sarah Jessica Parker Believes That Fragrances Have an
Important Mission in the World**

The key thing, actress Parker explains, is that perfumes
should have *social skills*. (No, we don't exactly get it either.)
But the horse-faced star is launching her own brand and
that is what she said. She explains:

"I think the beauty of the time we live in and where we
live is that everybody can walk into a room with different
political ideologies, with different religions, with different
thoughts about big themes and tiny themes and silly things.
And fragrance should be the same—it should have social
skills."

Okay, and how about athletic skills too?

**Mariah Carey Partners with Elizabeth Arden to Promote
"Timeless Values" via Bottles of Perfume**

Singer Mariah Carey joined with Elizabeth Arden in a
new perfume launch. But it was more than just that—it was
an important moment to express *timeless human values*. As
the chairman and chief executive of Elizabeth Arden ex-

plained: "We are thrilled to begin this partnership with Mariah Carey. She is, unquestionably, a star of incredible magnitude. All over the world, people aspire to the values she represents. We look forward to launching an inspiring new global fragrance brand with Mariah that will be a timeless classic."

One humble question: "The values she represents"?

Usher Brands Everything in Sight with His Name

Why stop with one product? This singer, who is producing a new line of watches with a watch designer, is not modest in his ambitions. In fact, he sounds maybe, just maybe, a tad *megalomaniacal.* "I want to brand everything that I do—a shirt that I wear, a pair of pants, the way I wear a combination of clothes."

Paris Hilton Introduces Her Latest Video Game Called "Diamondquest"—No, It's Not That, It's Uh, Called Uh, Something Else

Paris Hilton, a name quite naturally linked with the word "electronics," unveiled her new video game at the Los Angeles Electronic Entertainment Expo—which highlights the latest innovations in the video gaming industry.

Paris's quite unique personal innovation? *Calling her computer game by the wrong name*—and thereby confusing the competitors (and incidentally everyone else). "Sorry I'm late," the heiress said. "I'm really excited to have my new video game, 'Diamondquest.' Thank you all for coming, and you can download the game."

The problem was that the name of the game actually was "Paris Hilton's Jewel Jam." Seeing the similarities between the real name and "Diamondquest," though, one might say it was all just a natural mistake. (Note: Maybe to make it easier for Paris to remember, the company later changed the name to "Paris Hilton's Diamond Quest.")

Nicky Hilton Announces Hotel Chain with Clever Poster Board and Pasted Cutout Presentations

Most corporate product launches or presentations look professional—e.g., with PowerPoint presentations, overheads, slick lettering, etc. Most presentations worth over $100 million look even better. Unless you're Nicky Hilton and you're planning on launching a megaluxury hotel chain.

In that case, you use poster board, some cutouts, a few pictures—kind of like you were back in seventh grade and had to do a visual group project. More specifically, Nicky's stellar presentation appeared to center around collages on pink poster board, pictures of her, her clever logo (which is an *H*), what seemed to be a red Magic Marker drawing of a room, and two other boards with pictures clipped from magazines—a rug, a mirror and a table, and two gray posters—marked "Lobby" and "Lounge"—again with those magazine cutouts.

The "Nicky O" will offer condo units as well as transient lodging, with the condos starting at just under $500,000 and with penthouses priced at over $1 million. With a presentation like that, who can resist? We're buying.

Celebrities Tell Us How to Lose Millions

Being a celebrity product endorser is one of the top 10 easiest jobs in the world. All the celebrity has to do is stand there, project the right image, and occasionally talk about or wear the product—and get paid a ton. Simple enough.

But some celebrities get a little *challenged* when doing this.

Bye-bye, lucrative contract.

How to Lose a Lucrative Contract Technique #1: Fake an orgasm on a vibrating chair on Howard Stern's radio show.

Carmen Electra, hired by cosmetics giant Max Factor, was given strict rules regarding her behavior, the general idea being that she behave in a manner befitting a corporate spokesperson. Anyone with a few brain cells can figure out the basics of what would be acceptable and what wouldn't. For example, avoid riding sex machines on TV.

The *Baywatch* buxomity didn't get it, though. She went on Howard Stern and duly "rode" a sex machine live on the show. Helpfully, she also informed radio listeners she could get an orgasm from the gadget's vibrations. In fact, she was quite *enthusiastic* about it:

"It feels great. I have to get one for the house. It's awesome. This is the best thing I have ever felt in my life. I felt like I was going to take off."

This sexual product endorsement did not go over well with the corporate honchos at Max Factor, who informed Carmen that due to her behavior her entire contract with them was "under review." Carmen professed to be "shocked" at the company's reaction. She said: "I thought I didn't do anything wrong. I didn't do anything vulgar. It was a chair, I sat on a vibrating chair."

How to Lose a Lucrative Contract Technique #2: Don't mention or wear the clothes you're supposed to be promoting.

Here's an interesting technique: Get hired to promote some clothes—and then *never promote them*. This is what happened with Jessica Simpson, who signed a multimillion-dollar three-year licensing deal to launch a low-priced jean and clothing line for the Tarrant Apparel Group. In return for the millions, all Jessica had to do was wear the clothes and, like, *promote* the Tarrant clothing products, "JS by Jessica Simpson" and Princy jeans. You know: talk about them, wear them, be seen with them.

But for some unfathomable reason, Jessica couldn't do that—in fact, she even *refused* to be photographed wearing them.

And then . . . when she was asked at an event what was her favorite brand of jeans, instead of moving her lips carefully and remembering the right words and saying "Princy" (try it, it's not that hard, just two syllables—Prin-cee) she left out an *n* and said the *pricy* "True Religion" brand instead. The name of a *competitor*.

Bottom line: In April 2006, the Tarrant Group sued the not-so-astute actress/spokesperson for $100 million. As of this writing it seems she is still fighting it.

How to Lose a Lucrative Contract Technique #3:
Trash the clothes you're supposed to be promoting.

Jessica Simpson may seem to have reached the pinnacle of the "how to lose a contract for doing almost nothing by acting stupid," but then along came Christina Aguilera.

She was offered a multimillion-dollar contract to launch a celebrity line of clothing for Basic Box. Fair enough. But in an interview, the singer offered this interesting take on celebrity clothes lines: "They're tacky." She added something to the effect that she "would never even dream of launching her own clothing line since it would look like her singing career was over."

Basic Box seemed to agree that maybe Aguilera should focus on her singing contract after all. They canceled the clothing contract.

"I Am Not a Sellout": Celebrity Product Endorsements

Often celebrities get a tad . . . *defensive* . . . when asked about the millions they rake in from product endorsements. They feel beleaguered by the media, assailed by negative comments, and generally, *woefully* misunderstood.

See, the thing is, when celebs earn a little extra dough (say a few million here or there) from product endorsements, they definitely aren't doing it for the money. They are not that crass, nor so money-obsessed. They are doing it for bigger, deeper, more meaningful reasons.

Or so they say.

Defense #1: I'm endorsing this product to fulfill my childhood dream

Used By: Tennis star Venus Williams

Yes, some celebrities when young fantasized about the days when they could be associated with a product. (Of course. Don't we ALL do this when we're kids? You know, dream about plugging, say, a fast food chain? Yeah. Us neither.)

But Venus Williams did! (So did sis Serena, apparently.)

"As a child I always dreamed of becoming a McDonald's athlete," Venus says. So she has appeared in Mickey D ads (with pictures of salads and other lower-fat menu choices intercut with her on court running over lyrics like "I'm burnin' calories like a fiend. . . . Leafy greens so right for you. I'm making good choices, you can, too"). She does make appearances for the charitable Ronald McDonald House. And the lucky aspiring designer even designed a hat—a large, red newsboy cap with black designs and her signature on the inside label—for McDonald's employees to wear while serving food during the Olympics in Athens. It looked like, well, a large red newsboy hat. But we're *sure* that it was Venus's design ability that got her this particular gig.

Amount Paid for Fulfilling Said Childhood Dream: Roughly $3 million a year

Defense #2: I only chose *meaningful* endorsements
Used By: Ex-royal Sarah (Fergie) Ferguson, Duchess of York

Fergie knows from meaning. Faced with a cash crunch after she left the British royal family gravy train, the gutsy Sarah went out looking for work. But not just *any* work—work she could believe in. You know, sort of the way her fellow royal Princess Diana did promotional work against land mines. So Fergie went out there and found something that spoke to her: diet cranberry juice.

"I could have paid off my debts a lot quicker, but I only did things I actually believed in myself, like Cranberry Juice Lite," she explained.

Talk about your integrity!

Amount Paid for Endorsing the Meaningful Diet Drink: $845,000

Defense #3: The press is the one focusing on money, not me
Used By: Shaquille O'Neal

Quoth the weary Shaq: "I'm tired of hearing about money, money, money. I just want to play the game, drink Pepsi, and wear Reebok."

Yup, it's unfair as hell. So we'll just let his words speak for themselves. (And we're *sure* the fact that he happened to slip his two biggest product endorsements into his comment was because he really, truly just *loves* Pepsi. And Reebok.)

Wait—we should have said "loved," as in the past tense. Because now we have a hunch he isn't as nuts about Pepsi and Reebok, but really, truly just *loves* Swatch, Nestlé Crunch, Starter, Radio Shack, and Burger King. It's just a feeling we have (mainly since the Pepsi and Reebok deals are in the past).

Amount Paid for Believing in Soft Drinks and Sneakers: $25 million for Pepsi, $3 million (in 1992) for Reebok

Defense #4: I am following instructions from beyond the grave

Used By: Michael Jackson

Trust Michael to come up with the most novel reason for making money on product endorsement. See, Jackson owned the rights to a number of Beatles songs. And Nike wanted to use one in an ad. But Jackson wasn't sure if he should license the words and music of John Lennon's song "Revolution" to the sneaker manufacturer.

Luckily, John Lennon's ghost appeared to him! And, luckily, the spirit said, "Let my music live!" Jackson explained that he had "been thinking about the Nike ad all day. I immediately understood what he was telling me."

Amount Paid for Listening to Lennon's Ghost: A rather ethereal $250,000

Easy Money

Sometimes celebrities don't even have to endorse a product, slap their name on a perfume bottle, or whatever. They just have to *be* somewhere (or, in Mariah's case, go away somewhere). Great work if you can get it. . . .

CELEBRITY	WELL-EARNED PAYCHECK	HARD WORK REQUIRED	COMMENTS
Mariah Carey	$29 million	None	Virgin paid Carey the $29 million to buy out her contract —after her *Glitter* album (the first in a $100 million multirecord deal) bombed.
Model Marcus Schenkenberg	$5,000 a pop	Has to hang out in a Milan, Italy, nightclub	"I just wish I could do it more often."
Leonardo DiCaprio	$4 million	Two days of shooting a commercial for Orico, a Japanese credit card	
Justin Timberlake	Offered $1 million	Sing at the bar mitzvah of billionaire Philip Green's son	

CELEBRITY	WELL-EARNED PAYCHECK	HARD WORK REQUIRED	COMMENTS
Destiny's Child	$2.2 million	Sing at the bar mitzvah of billionaire Philip Green's son	
Paris Hilton	$200,000	Show up at a Cannes charity event	"All I had to do was wave like this," she said, demonstrating a beauty pageant contestant's wave.
Paris Hilton	$1 million	Show up at a Vienna charity event	"I had to say 'hi' and tell them why I loved Austria so much." So why does she like Austria? "Because they pay me $1 million to wave at crowds!"

7

CELEBRITY MONEY

"**I**'D RATHER NOT TALK about money. It's kind of gross," says Barbra Streisand, a woman acutely aware of its value.

Unfortunately, we're compelled to address this gross and disgusting subject since celebrities have so damn *much* of it.

Frugal or Cheap?: Celebrities Who Pinch Pennies

How, you may wonder, do celebrities have so much money? Part of it, of course, is due to their income. (Which is high.) But we suspect that another part of it may be due to their superior budgeting ability. Some people may call this "being frugal." Other less charitable types may call it "being cheap."

But what's the difference? One person's cheap is another person's frugal.

In the cases below of celebrities saving a few pennies, we'll carefully examine their fiscal behavior, in a completely neutral and objectively scientific manner, and then let you, the reader, answer our question:

Was this celebrity being fabulously *frugal* . . . or criminally *cheap*?

Potentially Cheap Celebrity #1: Barbra Streisand
Potentially Cheap Action: Avoiding valet parking

On December 2, 2002, Streisand and hubby James Brolin, meeting people at the L.A. restaurant Ago, drove past the restaurant in an effort to find parking space on the street—instead of paying the $3.50 valet parking fee.

Potentially Cheap Savings: Streisand's net worth is estimated by *Forbes* to be around $100 million. Thus, driving around to avoid paying $3.50 amounts to seeking a savings of .0000000001% of her total fortune.

So was this free parking quest **frugal** or **cheap**?

Potentially Cheap Celebrity #2: Katie Couric
Potentially Cheap Action: Searching out and buying $1 panties from the discount bin

Potentially Cheap Savings: Since the average Victoria's Secret panty costs about $10, let's assume our penny-pinching serio-cutesie newsreader Katie saves around $9 per panty. Katie was making around $13 million a year at the time she was observed in her $1 panty quest, which is roughly $250,000 a week, or around $4,166 an hour (assuming a generous 60-hour week), which comes to $69 a minute. Thus, her discount savings of $9 per panty represents about eight seconds of personal work time.

So is her bargain panty scouting **frugal** or **cheap**?

Potentially Cheap Celebrity #3: Tyra Banks
Potentially Cheap Action: In her own words: "If people come to my house and don't finish their water, I'll write their name on the bottle and give it to them when they come back."

Potentially Cheap Savings: The exact amount saved of

course depends on 1) the type of bottled water and 2) how much is left. Let's assume an average guest drinks half the bottled water; and for the sake of argument, let's pick a well-known brand, say, Fiji water. Each bottle would cost 90.6 cents (presuming she is buying her Fiji water by the case *and* on sale for $26.50 per 24 bottles). *Forbes* says she made $6 million in 2005—so by not offering her guests a *fresh* bottle of Fiji, Tyra is saving .0000001% of her annual salary!

So is her water conservation **frugal** or **cheap**?

Potentially Cheap Celebrity #4: Julia Roberts

Potentially Cheap Action: Trying to bargain down a cheap vintage frock from $65 to $20 at a flea market

Potentially Cheap Savings: Note that the savings in this case are only theoretical, since the flea market vendor didn't budge from his price, pointing out that he had to earn a living, too. However, let's figure out how much Roberts would have saved had the vendor yielded to her bargaining powers. Since Roberts had just recently bought a $6.4 million home in Malibu, as well as the adjoining land for $14 million, we'll figure out the potential savings as a percentage of Roberts's most recent real estate purchases. The bargain clothing price she was seeking was $45 lower than the asking price, for a potential savings of $45 versus the $20,400,000 of her local real estate holdings, or in percentage terms, 0.0000022% of the value of her real estate; about the cost of maybe a few weeds and a Malibu rock.

Was Julia's $45 bargaining session **frugal** or **cheap**?

Potentially Cheap Celebrity #5: Singer Charlotte Church

Potentially Cheap Action: Buying sofas on the credit plan, 12 months interest free

Potentially Cheap Savings: Charlotte bought the two sofas costing $10,324 for her new $938,000 home. Charlotte said: "Why not take advantage of a good offer? I think the salesman thought we were joking at first but I insisted on the credit-free option." By not paying cash and letting the company give her an interest-free loan for a year, Charlotte, in effect, earned an extra $485.22 (assuming she invested the money in an interest-bearing CD paying 4.7%—the rough average at the time). A nice addition to her $17,200,000 annual income in 2006!

Was this **frugal** or **cheap**?

Potentially Cheap Celebrity #6: Dr. Phil
Potentially Cheap Action: Cut-rate pay to employees
Potentially Cheap Savings: The good doctor—whose personal pay scale topped $45 million from June 2005 to June 2006, according to *Forbes*—recently advertised for transcribers for his syndicated TV show. The pay offered? $7 an hour . . . and no benefits. Added perk: Employees must be willing to work the graveyard shift. Here's an interesting comparison: using the figure above, we estimate that Dr. Phil makes $21,634 per hour (assuming a 40-hour work week). His transcribers would be making $14,560 a *year*.

Was this **frugal** or **cheap**?

Potentially Cheap Celebrity #7: Britney Spears
Potentially Cheap Action: Making loved one fly discount
Potentially Cheap Savings: Spears, just before marrying the self-styled "rapper" Kevin Federline, traveled with him across the Atlantic. As befits a star, Spears chose to fly first-class. As befits a, well, something else, Federline was not given the same option. Observers saw Federline wait-

ing patiently in the first-class line with his beloved, and further watched as he then repaired to the economy line. Did Federline mind the cramped quarters while she-who-must-be-obeyed was lolling in first class? Not at all! He reportedly anesthetized himself with eight rum and Cokes on the 10-hour flight. Meanwhile, by our estimate, the Spears/Federline family saved roughly $6,635 (the difference between first class and economy on a recent British Airways one-way flight)—which would easily cover more than eight rum and Cokes.

Was this **frugal** or **cheap**?

Potentially Cheap Celebrity #8: Fred Durst, the Limp Bizkit frontman

Potentially Cheap Action: Using 5% electronics store discount

Potentially Cheap Savings: There are discounts and there are discounts. Durst's record company has a 5% discount at a certain electronics store, and quite reasonably takes advantage of it. However, it was recently reported that the multimillionaire rocker demanded, and got, this 5% discount when purchasing a $20 iPod cable, saving himself all of $1. PR reps for Durst did not return a call asking for further elaboration of his fiscal prudence.

Was this **frugal** or **cheap**?

Answers: 1. Cheap 2. Cheap 3. Cheap 4. Cheap 5. Cheap 6. Cheap 7. Cheap (but understandable—this way she didn't have to sit next to K-Fed) 8. Frugal (Given Limp Bizkit's rather limp album sales post-2003, maybe Fred needs to save that buck. But if you want to call it cheap, that's okay too.)

Necessary Expenses—or, "If You've Got It, Flaunt It!"

PURCHASER	WHAT WAS BOUGHT	HOW MUCH THEY SPENT	WHY IT WAS WORTH IT
Britney Spears	Chinese scissors to cut her hair	$3,000	These are *special* scissors, of course.
Singer Tommy Lee	Starbucks franchise (so he could put a Starbucks in the house for his then-wife Pam Anderson)	$4,000	Pam loved Starbucks, Tommy Lee loved Pam.
Sting	Christmas tree	$11,900	It's *Christmas,* dammit!
Terence Howard	Man-purse	$34,000	Diamonds, alligator, and all man. What more can you ask for in a man-purse?
Nicky Hilton and actor **Kevin Connolly**	Bottle of Cristal	$100,000	Needed something special to drink on New Year's Eve
Sean "Diddy" Combs	Rented a yacht for Mediterranean vacation	$800,000	Had gold-plated faucets and the ever-necessary helicopter pad

8

THE TRAVELING CELEBRITY

CELEBRITIES SPEND A LOT of time in airplanes (forced to travel first-class when their private jets aren't available), in expensive hotels (forced to "rough it" in presidential suites), and in exclusive restaurants.

You think they'd be grateful for all their first-class treatment? (Insert hollow laugh here.) You think they'd be nice to the flight attendants, fellow passengers, waiters, and hotel clerks? (Insert another hollow laugh.) You think they'd act like rational, polite human beings?

Guess again, sucka.

The "Bad Behavior in the Air" Awards

As special members of our traveling society, celebrities set the standards for safe, civilized air travel. But do they ever get recognized for their achievements in the air? Sadly, no.

We've decided to rectify this matter and offer the first-ever "Bad Behavior in the Air" Awards—or, as we like to call them, the Airheads.

The envelope please . . .

The "Who Says Traveling with an Infant Is Difficult?" Award goes to . . . Maria Shriver, news "journalist" personality and wife of movie star and governor Arnold Schwarzenegger

During an airplane trip some ten or more years ago Maria was flying first-class; baby and nanny were deposited in coach. When the Shriver baby started wailing and crying and in general disturbing the other coach passengers, the nanny went forward to find Maria in first class, hoping she, as the mother, could help calm the squalling infant. Maria's response? "She's your problem." Sending the nanny back, this paragon of "nothing bothers me" traveling motherhood proceeded to take a nap.

The "Why Pay Full Fare for the Whole Family?" Award goes to . . . Jean-Claude Van Damme, aging action star

On a British Airways flight from Cannes, Van Damme bought a first-class ticket for himself, business class for wife and kids. Once the plane took off, however, Van Damme loudly demanded that his family be permitted to join him in first class. His reason? Should the airplane crash, he wished to be able to "hold hands" with them. The BA flight crew was not swayed by this line of reasoning, but in a spirit of compromise, allowed the actor's son (but not his wife and daughter) to join his cheapskate father in first class. Passengers were also not impressed by Van Damme's logic. As one passenger commented, "Look, pal, if you want to fly first class, just pay for it."

The "It's Party Time" Award goes to . . . Lara Flynn Boyle, actress best known for starring in *Twin Peaks*, being thin, and dating Jack Nicholson

According to fellow passengers on an L.A. to London flight, Lara partook of a few too many unidentified pills and a number of alcoholic drinks. Following this Ms. Boyle became "wild-eyed" and then left her seat. The object of her leaving was evidently a sleeping male passenger, whom the wild-eyed starlet attempted to join in his sleeping berth. Alert crew members managed to put a towel around Ms. Boyle and escort her back to her seat, where she showed her displeasure by ripping out the reading light. Later, getting up to go to the bathroom, a perhaps contrite Ms. Boyle very kindly flashed the staff.

The "Sweet Smell of Excess" Award goes to . . . Britney Spears

On a recent cross-country flight with her then-husband, superstar Britney decided to 1) kick back, 2) relax, and 3) take off her shoes. The problem was with Britney's third act. Shortly thereafter, everyone in first class was aware of an absolutely disgusting yet telltale odor emanating from Britney's seat, or more specifically, from her feet.

After hearing complaints, crew members approached the smelly star and asked that she please put her shoes back on. The star complied, but hardly in a way to win new friends or fans: "These shoes are so comfortable, but they always make my feet stink," she said.

Apparently her fellow passengers were neither amused nor sympathetic.

The "Fun Fellow Passengers" Award goes to . . . Tom Snyder, former TV talk-show host

During a turbulent airplane flight, the talk show host apparently began shouting: "This is it! No one will come out alive! We're all doomed!"

One celebrity flier who wins the award for least annoying—or at least quietest—passenger in recent history: Bono's hat. U2 singer Bono—caught in Italy without his favorite hat—did what any hat lover would do: shelled out $1,700 to have his hat flown to him. First class.

Celebrity Hotel Guests from Hell: "Normal" Celebrity Hotel Requests

Once a celebrity lands, it's off to a posh hotel—where he or she will happily exasperate and aggravate harried hotel staffers via persnickety, preposterous, and presumptuous hotel needs.

Celebrity Guest: Jennifer Lopez
Chief Hotel Need: A sea of white

God forbid Jennifer spend a night in a room with pink . . . or yellow . . . or even beige. Everything—*everything*—has to be white. She insists that the suite be freshly painted white. Furniture must be white too, and the room must be filled with white lilies and roses and (white) scented candles—preferably perfumed with Diptych.

Other Hotel Needs: Sheets (white, natch) must be Egyptian cotton with thread counts of at least 250; room temperature must be set at exactly (EXACTLY!) 25.5 degrees Celsius/80 degrees Fahrenheit

Celebrity Guest: Mary J. Blige

Chief Hotel Need: No interruptions whatsoever—and she means it (to the tune of 26 exclamation points on the rider she sends to hotels)

It's all spelled out in the document her folks send to hotels—housekeepers must pay attention to her DO NOT DISTURB sign; and there can be no noise in the hallway—vacuums, etc. If the hotel plans any "construction or redecorating . . . in or near the hotel," the hotel has to pay for relocation.

Other Hotel Needs: Presidential suite with brand new toilet seat

Celebrity Guest: Justin Timberlake

Chief Hotel Need: Privacy . . . and disinfectant

No germs for JT! He insists that new air conditioner filters be in place upon his arrival and, more important, that *all* door handles be disinfected every few hours. In addition, heaven forbid that a housekeeper talk to him. His hotel rider specifies that the hotel staff may under no circumstances address him. (We are not sure if this rule can be broken if a staffer wants to warn him about possible E coli or other infestations.)

Other Hotel Needs: Extra-large stereo unit, Nintendo PlayStation, fitness studio (private, of course)

Celebrity Guest: Madonna

Chief Hotel Need: Spiritually sound room—at any cost

You're a guest, you need to do your yoga and meditate and generally be spiritually amazing . . . so *naturally* you ask to have your $850-per-night room painted just the right shade of warm orange to facilitate said spiritual shit, right? Well, then, you must be Madonna! She demanded that her room at the Grand Hotel in Stockholm, Sweden, be re-painted so as to supply her with the right spiritual atmo-sphere.

Other Hotel Needs: Personal items, which she brings in by the truckload; cases of specific Kaballah water (blessed by Jewish mystics) to drink—which, sadly, isn't that easy to get in Europe. Said one source, "It would be easier if Madonna just demanded expensive Champagne, like all the other spoiled celebrities."

Celebrity Guest: Tara Reid
Chief Hotel Need: Extra room

Tara was in Europe—shooting her reality TV show that has since bitten the dust, for some reason that escapes us—when she and Paris Hilton booked rooms at London's Baglioni Hotel. One might have thought that a posh $2,000-a-night suite would be of ample size, but not for Tara! She asked for a second room . . . to keep her shoes in. A source told the *Daily Telegraph,* "It was absolutely bizarre. She said she'd collected all these shoes while she'd been traveling around Europe, but quite why she has to house them separately remains a mystery. The irony is that Miss Hilton was also staying but she was no trouble at all."

Celebrity Guest: Eminem
Chief Hotel Need: Rough equivalent of McDonald's, Taco Bell, etc.

Eminem is just a down-home kinda guy . . . which is why he insists upon down-home kinda hotel care. His main request: whatever kind of fast food exists in the country. You can take the boy out of Detroit, but you can't take De-troit out of the boy. . . .

Other Hotel Needs: Personal masseuse, PlayStation, Ping-Pong table

Celebrity Guest: Mariah Carey

Chief Hotel Need: Proper recognition of her importance and, indeed, glory

Mariah expects the red carpet treatment . . . literally. God forbid she has to set a dainty foot on plain old pavement. Case in point: Carey and entourage were pulling up to the Baglioni Hotel in London when she was met with a shock: Hotel staffers unbelievably had forgotten to roll out the red carpet flanked by large white candles—at 2:15 in the morning. The shocked star was forced to drive around the block in a parade of limos until the offending sidewalk was appropriately covered . . . and she could finally go to her room. In addition to a red carpet, Carey insists upon gold fixtures in the suite—and a new toilet seat installed before her arrival.

Other Hotel Needs: 2 DVD players—playing only her videos; French mineral water in suite for both herself and her dog to bathe in; has own sheets and pillows flown in

TRAVELING INCOGNITO

Pity the poor celebrity! Plagued by shutter-snapping paparazzi, pushy tabloid reporters, and overzealous fans, they can't just march up to a hotel reservation desk and give their name. (Well, they *can* . . . but that's not the point here.)

No, many times they prefer to travel incognito, using an alias. But do they pick dull, run-of-the-mill, easily overlooked names like "John Peterson" or "Melissa Berg"?

Heavens no!

The aliases: Tarquin Budgerigar, Bobo Latrine, Jr., Binky Poodle-Clip, Sir Horace Pussy

The incognito star: Elton John

The circumstances: While Elton was staying under the name Sir Horace Pussy at a hotel, the operator refused to put through a call from his mother. She was less than amused. Finally she was forced to admit her own identity: "But I am *MRS.* Pussy," quoth she.

The alias: Bryce Pilaf

The incognito star: Brad Pitt

The circumstances: Just after his then-wife Jennifer Aniston filed for divorce, Pitt checked into a Palm Springs hotel (as did co-star and rumored lover Angelina Jolie). Pitt gets extra points not for using a food as a name, but for using his own initials in said fake name. This is a technique often recommended by private investigators.

The aliases: Mr. Poopy, Emma Roid, Mr. Stench (but *not* Mr. Donkey Penis, as has been reported)

The incognito star: Johnny Depp

The circumstances: Depp claims he uses ostensibly humorous aliases due to his puckish sense of humor. As he put it: "It's just that if you register as Mr. Poopy, for instance, you get a funny wake-up call. I used to use the name Mr. Stench; it was funny to be in a posh hotel and hear a very proper concierge call out, 'Mr. Stench, please!' I never really stayed under the name Donkey Penis. That was an example I mentioned to a reporter once."

"I'll Have That with a Side of Ego, Please": Five Celebrity Restaurant Crimes, and a Few Misdemeanors

Celebrities are just like us—by which we mean that they eat. Food. And often they eat said food in restaurants.

Unlike us, though, they sometimes do . . . things . . . in restaurants that we wouldn't do. (Well, we're not sure about you, actually.) Let's put it another way: They do things in restaurants that might get mere morals like us kicked out, banned forever, arrested, and so on.

We can only assume they think they're so *special* that it never *ever* occurs to them that maybe one oughtn't do certain things. Things we consider absolutely *criminal* in the context of a restaurant.

Like what?

Read on.

Celeb Restaurant Perp: Britney Spears
Crime: Changing baby's poopy diaper at table

Having a baby didn't stop mommy Britney Spears from enjoying a nice meal at a posh Beverly Hills restaurant. She just brought little Sean Preston with her. And having the baby poop in his diaper *still* didn't stop her from enjoying that meal. She just changed him.

Right at the table.

More specifically, she put the baby on her table (which was, of course, an *eating* table, not a changing table), removed the laden diaper (which was, of course, a little . . . pong-y, let us say), and put a new one on—all amidst the crystal and silverware . . . and the other diners.

These paying patrons were not terribly thrilled by this exhibition of the gastrointestinal system in action. "It was disgusting. Someone else has got to eat at that table! Yuck," said one. The manager was more than a little gobsmacked himself, but, as he said to a complaining diner, "It's Britney Spears—what can we do?"

(Note: Britney has a propensity for laissez-faire diaper

changing. While buying some undies at a Victoria's Secret in Mission Viejo, California, Britney squatted down on the floor by the cash register and—no, she didn't poop—changed Sean P.'s poopy diaper, and tried to hand it to the salesperson. The salesperson did not take it.)

Celeb Restaurant Perp: Demi Moore
Crime: Preventing other patrons from using only bathroom in restaurant—for over half an hour

Demi Moore was at a hot L.A. restaurant when she got up from her table, went to the only bathroom, and locked herself in. And there she stayed for over half an hour.

Poor Demi! A bad oyster gave her the runs? She was touched with a little tummy problem? Presumably not, since people trying to get into the lone toilet could hear her on the phone, but could hear no other sounds of intestinal distress.

When finally she got out of the bathroom, a hostile group confronted her (presumably with their legs pressed tightly together). She had a good reason for being in the bathroom, she explained. Like, duh! It was her daughter's bedtime and she was talking her into going to bed.

Celeb Restaurant Perp: Kiefer Sutherland
Crime: Suspicious behavior involving karate kicks, missing wallets, and copious consumption of alcohol

Kiefer Sutherland wandered into the tiny Ye Rustic Inn in Los Angeles, insisted on starting a tab, and ordered a round of drinks for himself and a loud group of friends.

Oh, did we mention it was 9:00 A.M. when he walked in? You know, shank of the evening and all that . . .

When the bartender gave him a bill, ol' Kief got a little upset. His wallet was "indisposed," as he said. "It's been stolen! I promise I'll come back and pay." And it went downhill from there. He then started doing karate kicks in the middle of the floor for the "entertainment" of the staff and the few customers in there. Happily, a fan bought him a few scotches and some chicken wings—which Kiefer threw back and ate, respectively, leaving the chicken bones artistically scattered on the floor. He left without tipping— a given due to that "indisposed" wallet, we guess.

Sutherland's representative had no comment on the morning festivities, but it was later reported that Sutherland and friends were just having one more for the road after having spent the night partying at the bar across the street.

Celeb Restaurant Perp: Naomi Campbell
Crime: Excessive toast-related pickiness

Toast is rarely a problem. Yes, it can be too dark or too light, but even these seem to be relatively minor issues. But Naomi Campbell would disagree with this.

She ordered a sandwich at Le Grand Véfour in Paris— and was "forced" to send it back. The problem? The toast was "scratching" her gums.

Celeb Restaurant Perp: Ashlee Simpson
Crime: Irritating behavior at fast food restaurant

Ashlee Simpson wandered into a Toronto area McDonald's, presumably for some fine dining, when she decided to act "silly and crazy," as she later put it. (Others preferred the word "drunk," but who are we to judge?)

Anyway, Ashlee was there, and so was a fan with a video camera—who caught her on tape calling the McDonald's counter clerk a "bitch" (how silly! how crazy!) and betting her $5 million that the manager would be nicer to her. The tape also showed her talking with a young man behind her, and sillily and crazily telling him to fuck off because he wouldn't kiss her foot. And she got on the counter as well. Right where a Happy Meal would be.

Ashlee defended herself by saying that the tape had been edited to make her look bad. She claimed that "the guy in line behind me was like, 'Uh, you're gross' but he didn't know who I was until I turned around. Then he was like, 'Can I have my picture with you?' and I was like, 'Dude, you called me gross!' "

And *we're* like, how silly and crazy!

Misdemeanor citations for irritating celebrity/restaurant moments go to:

- **Jennifer Lopez,** for sending in members of her security team to check out London's posh restaurant the Ivy— before she would deign to dine. (Sources claim that the restaurant was not amused by J Lo's uber-security consciousness and asked her to dine elsewhere.)

- **Lindsay Lohan,** for just acting bitchy. The teen queen flounced into the Saddle Ranch Chop House in Universal City with five female pals and did it up, diva-style. First, she hated her table, and insisted on being moved to another. Second, she got snappy with the waiter when she ordered. Third, she sent her food back. And, for her final act, she left a less-than-queenly $2 tip.

- **Demi Moore** (again) and her then-hubby Bruce Willis, for eating their meal at a costly L.A. restaurant on the floor. Under the table. Oh, they were so cute and wacky back then, weren't they? You never hear about Demi and Ashton doing things like this!

9

CELEBRITY LOVE AND MARRIAGE (AND SEX TOO)

CELEBRITIES, SEX, AND ROMANCE are synonymous. Who hasn't imagined a sexy tryst with some hot star or a whirl-wind romantic interlude with a rocker in Ibiza?

Actually, we hope you haven't. It shows you have good taste.

Stars Answer Your Love and Sex Questions

Confused about romance? Not getting enough? You might want to do what a lot of other people do nowadays: ask a celebrity. (Why anyone should care what they think is beyond us, but what the hey.)

Q: What's the perfect icebreaker when you're beginning a relationship?
JENNY MCCARTHY: "Just fart right away."

Q: Should you kiss with your eyes open or closed?
JESSICA SIMPSON: "I love to kiss with my eyes open, because I can take in the entire situation and know if I'm enjoying it or not."

Q: What makes a man sexy?

YASMINE BLEETH: "I love a man who can wear my underwear."

Q: How do you know if she's Ms. Right?

NICOLAS CAGE: "When she showed up at my house dressed head to toe in black vinyl, carrying a big purple wedding cake, I knew I was with the right woman."

Q: Is it okay to cheat?

PARIS HILTON: "When you're in the public eye, it's wrong to cheat on someone, unless you're very careful. If you're normal and no one's going to know, then do it."

Q: How can you tell if it's time to break up with someone?

SAMAIRE ARMSTRONG: "I feel like if I'm sick, I need flowers. I'm very open about saying what I need from a partner, and he needs to meet those demands. I got my wisdom teeth pulled, and I guess maybe I expected a little bit more support. That was just the straw that broke the camel's back. If you're not going to be there for my wisdom teeth, you're not going to be there."

Q: Do looks really matter?

BILLY BOB THORNTON: "Sometimes with the model, the actress, or the 'sexiest person in the world,' it may literally be like fucking the couch." (Note: Billy Bob's ex, Angelina Jolie, was once named *Esquire*'s "Sexiest Person in the World.")

CAN'T YOU USUALLY TELL THE DIFFERENCE?

Scarlett Johansson admitted that she and Benicio Del Toro were spotted getting hot and heavy in an elevator at the Chateau Marmont hotel after the Oscars: "We were making out or having sex or something, which I think is very unsanitary."

Celebrities Share Their Sexual Secrets by Several Standard Deviations of Information More Than We Want to Know

Some celebrities' sexual secrets should be just that. Secret. Please, God . . .

Sexual Secret: I just LOVE golden showers.
Generous Sexual Secrets Contributor: Singer Ricky Martin

"I love giving the golden shower. I've done it before in the shower. It's like so sexy, you know, the temperature of your body and the shower water is very different."

(Very interesting and clearly knowledgeable point about the different relative temperatures of urine and shower water.)

Sexual Secret: I've got a ring—no, not on my finger but on my . . .
Generous Sexual Secrets Contributor: Rocker Lenny Kravitz

IS BRAD PITT TAKING JUJU HERBS TO GIVE HIM THE STRENGTH OF THE LION?

Maybe so . . . if reports from Kenya are true. One night on safari, Brad and Angelina Jolie were making love so loudly that "it sounded like a wounded animal, like someone being killed." According to one source, "Africans have great respect for men with sexual prowess. Miss Jolie got so excited during sex the guards thought maybe Mr. Pitt was taking magic juju herbs to give him the strength of a lion."

"It's a hoop about the size of a quarter—it hits the lady where she likes it."

(We'll tell all the ladies, Len.)

Sexual Secret: After having sex with Paris Hilton, I washed my gonads with a household cleaning product.

Generous Sexual Secrets Contributor: Elijah Blue Allman, son of Cher and rocker Gregg Allman

Elijah revealed to Howard Stern on his radio show that he had had sex with Paris Hilton—before she was famous. But afterward he got worried that the allegedly promiscuous star might be harboring an STD, so he raced downstairs and poured a household cleaning product over his possibly infected organs to "disinfect" them.

Hilton, upon hearing of this pubic—uh, public—airing of the aftermath of his sex act with her, was "not happy about it," according to a source.

SEX SECRETS OF THE X-MEN

It must be something about the X-Men . . . Hugh Jackman's wife likes him to wear his Wolverine costume in bed—for a little added kink. "I feel a bit silly in that outfit but, believe me, my wife really, really likes it. They'll have to make a new one for the next movie because she won't let me part with it."

And Halle Berry likes wearing her Storm costume when she's in bed too. "Yeah, I wear it sometimes. You gotta keep your life spiced up. Storm never has sex in the movies—but Storm has a lotta sex at my house."

No word on the sex habits of Beast or Nightcrawler.

(But Elijah, ever the gentleman, also reported that Paris was a "sweet girl." Even if he thought her nether regions harbored potentially lethal pathogens.)

Sexual Secret: I shave my gray hair; yeah, down there, my pubies.
Generous Sexual Secrets Contributor: Rocker Billy Idol

"I shaved my balls—they were going gray, so I shaved them. It's like steel wool down there!"

(Thanks for sharing that description of your gonadal area, Billy. It'll always be there for us.)

Sexual Secret: Do you want to hear how I masturbate? Do you?
Generous Sexual Secrets Contributor: Jim Carrey

"I believe in staying in balance . . . I do masturbate, but not like a fiend."

(Thank GOD!)

"He's *Such* a Gentleman!": Celeb Guys Any Gal Would Just Adore

Hollywood has long had a love affair with "bad boys"— those guys who ride hogs, don't talk much, and treat women like dirt. But what about all those good guys out there? Don't they deserve to be applauded for their gentlemanly behavior? Yes, say we!

Herewith, then, some awards for male celebrities who are truly heckuva guys. The kind of guy you'd love to take home to meet Mom. Frankly, we can't say enough about them.

Really. We can't.

The "I Get a Kick from Champagne" Award goes to . . . rapper 50 Cent . . . who wants to encourage women to reach new heights of sexual ecstasy—via drink-induced threesomes and/or orgies

50 Cent just *loves* the new law instituted in England that allows pubs to be open 24 hours a day. No, he's not that heavy a drinker. He just likes the odds. "England's drinking laws are definitely going to cause more threesomes—and if you're out that late, you gotta feed the girl the Champagne. They love that stuff," he told Britain's (aptly named) *Loaded* magazine. He apparently speaks from experience since he added, "Man, I've had some good times and parties in pubs after 11 pm." But Fitty is a careful bon vivant. He made sure

to add that "everyone should use a condom, because more drinking will also cause more baby population."

The "I Feel Your Pain" Award goes to . . . singer Rod Stewart (in a twofer!) . . . who oh-so-sensitively and kindly breaks up with women

Talk about your sweethearts! Back when he was a serial charmer, Stewart apparently cared enough to not leave a gal dangling, wondering where the relationship was going. Mr. Sensitive realized that it's better to be up front and sensitive: "I've always been the one to push and shove and say, 'Sorry, that's it darlin', it's all over, goodbye. Take twenty Valiums and have a stomach pump and that's the end of it.'"

. . . and who also sensitively and kindly pointed out past dumpees to his then-wife

AND . . . since Rod slept with so many women, he tried to be on his toes to avoid embarrassing his wife. "It's impossible for me to remember everybody I've made love to . . . I try and point them out if Rachel and I are out together and we bump into somebody I've dated before," said Stewart while boasting about his honest relationship with then 22-year-old wife Rachel Hunter. (In a happy twist of poetic justice, Hunter wound up dumping Stewart.)

The "Warm and Fuzzy" Award goes to . . . aging genius actor (IQ 180) James Woods . . . for cutely explaining that happiness is a warm (and preferably well-endowed) puppy

Woods (IQ 180) has long been a fan of younger women. When he was a mere child of 52, he appeared on *Access Hollywood* to answer the perplexing question: Why do so many Hollywood actors hook up with younger women? His answer:

"Look, let me ask you something. Did you ever buy a dog? You got a puppy when you bought a dog. You didn't buy a 13-year-old German shepherd. You wanna buy? You wanna buy a nice young puppy."

And what does a puppy—er, excuse us, we mean a young woman—think of this? Let's listen to his then-fiancée Melissa Crider—who was 25, or less than half of her soul mate's age, at the time:

"Jimmy's—you know—very fun. Uh—I think I'm the luckiest girl in the world. I—I really—uh—I'm really attracted to—[long pause]—to wisdom."

So clearly it wasn't just her looks that attracted him to her . . . right?

The "Susan B. Anthony Award for Enlightened Male Thought" goes to . . . the ever-roguish Charlie Sheen . . . who has shown a history of clearly evolved views on women and relationships

Charlie is prone to using interesting object names for women—inanimate, at that. But, well, let's just let Charlie speak for himself here:

"Why settle for hamburger when you can have prime rib?"

> —CHARLIE, explaining why he has a porn star for a girl-friend

"He is spiritual!"

> —then-girlfriend porn star GINGER ALLEN (clearly appreciating Charlie's feminist streak)

"I had a girlfriend, but I got that piano off my back."

> —CHARLIE

"You buy a bad car, it breaks down, what are you gonna do?"

> —CHARLIE, in an *Entertainment Tonight* segment talking about his breakup with former wife, model Donna Peele

The "Neocons Can Be Wild and Crazy Guys Too!" Award goes to . . . formerly bow-tied, still boyish-faced TV pundit/wild dancer Tucker Carlson . . . for proving that believing in conservative doctrine doesn't mean you're conservative about women or sex

Tucker is one of those talking heads you often see on TV, opining about Iraq or Mideast peace in general, not to mention other weighty topics when he's not busting a move on that celebrity dance show. He's a fun guy! With fun attitudes about women! And he's open-minded!

For example, yes, he's a conservative, but he admits there are *good* things about liberals. To wit:

> "One area of liberal phenomenon I support is female bisexuality—this apparent increased willingness of girls to bring along a friend. That's a pretty good thing."

Ha ha ha! Once you wind this party (Grand Old, that is) animal up, he just doesn't quit.

> "[Women] want to be listened to, protected and amused. And they want to be spanked vigorously every once in a while."

But seriously, folks—if Tucker could be any woman, what woman would he be? Elizabeth Birch of the Human

Rights Campaign. And why? Because "you'd be presiding over an organization of thousands of lesbians, some of them quite good-looking."

You're just *such* a man, Tuck!

The "I'm a Stickler for Accuracy" Award goes to . . . golden oldie long-tongued geriatric rocker Gene Simmons . . . for insisting that the record be set straight on his alleged "bad boy" activities with groupies

Simmons wants to make sure that all those rumors about his alleged raunchy treatment of groupies are quashed once and for all. "There are so many myths about what I have done with girls on the road," he said, adding that he wanted people to know the *truth,* not the ramped-up versions that have been tossed about.

So what *really* happened during all those much talked about sexcapades, back when he was a wild rocker as opposed to merely an old one?

> "With this one lady, we were on the second floor of the Fairmont Hotel in San Francisco, and you can ask a beautiful girl who is naked almost anything and if she is in the right frame of mind, she will do it. As Machiavelli said, to have power is to abuse it, so I said to her, 'Climb out to the end of that flagpole naked. I want to take a picture of you instead of the flag.' And she did, naked."

Now isn't that much better than anything you might have heard? Wait, there's more . . .

> "Another time a girl was talking too loud and she would not shut up, so I gaffer-taped her mouth shut

and gaffer-taped her to a chair and then sent her down to the lobby in the elevator naked."

We're glad to have cleared things up.

The "Modesty Thy Name Is Wilmer" Award goes to . . . often-dated-for-reasons-that-escape-us actor Wilmer Valderrama . . . for thoughtfully sharing the wonderful qualities of women he's known with a national audience

Good-hearted Wilmer wants everyone to know how *great* certain women are. He's all about giving credit where credit is due, apparently. So, while on Howard Stern's satellite radio show, Wilmer was complimenting or otherwise sharing info on some of the boldfaced names he has been with. According to the Big W (so-named here because, on the same show, the modest star just happened to mention that he was "blessed" with a penis "slightly bigger" than eight inches): Ashlee Simpson is as loud in bed as she is on stage. Lindsay Lohan was one of the best in bed. As for her breasts? "They were real." It was "really good" to take Mandy Moore's virginity. He also let slip that he's been involved in threesomes and had anal sex with one actress—whom he politely didn't name. Oh, and sex with Jennifer Love Hewitt was an eight out of ten.

Jennifer Love Hewitt, however, says she and Valderrama never were lovers, never even dated, and were only friends. Some women just can't take a compliment, can they?

(Important note: The humble Wilmer also admitted that he had been rejected by women, but couldn't remember a specific instance.)

Honorable Mentions go to:

• Actor/*Jackass* star **Johnny Knoxville,** for proving that he's no jackass when it comes to having a good time.

He has priorities, dammit! And they showed when the then-34-year-old went out on the town in New Orleans with the then-18-year-old Lindsay Lohan and a group of friends. When they arrived at a local nightclub, the underage Lohan wasn't allowed inside. So "gentleman" Johnny left her outside and went inside to par-tay.

• Actor **Ben Affleck,** for his adorable sense of fun involving genitalia (his). While filming a shot of a briefcase in *Surviving Christmas* with Christina Applegate, he showed off his puckish side by placing his penis and balls on the case, so Christina could get a happy giggle. On the set of another film, *Jersey Girl,* the whimsical Affleck used to rest his scrotum on the back of director Kevin Smith's neck during filming breaks.

• **Sylvester Stallone** (the self-described "Hiroshima of Love")—for being ever-so-*moderne* when breaking up with his ex, model Angie Everhart. He sent a short and sweet rejection slip to her fax machine.

• Actor and sometime pugilist **Mickey Rourke**—for forthrightly explaining what a real sweet guy looks for in a woman. "It's like when I buy a horse. I don't want a thick neck and short legs."

The Most Romantic Gifts Ever Given by Celebrities

Say it with flowers, the ads say on Valentine's Day, but celebrities know that romance is sexier if the gifts are more *creative.* Let us see what celebrities reportedly gave their significant others:

Celebrity: Billy Bob Thornton to Angelina Jolie

Lovely Romantic Gift: Certificate drawn up that pledges never to leave her for eternity, with the seal of the great state of Louisiana on it, signed in his own blood with a paintbrush

Comment: Relationship lasted considerably less than any number of years approaching eternity, namely three.

Celebrity: Billy Bob Thornton to Angelina Jolie

Lovely Romantic Gift: Vial of blood

Comment: Somewhat surprised by the popular reaction to this self-perceived romantic Valentine-red gift, the actor commented: "If Michelle Pfeiffer gave Mel Gibson a vial of blood to wear around his neck in a movie you'd think it was terribly romantic, everyone would cry and they'd win awards. But in real life if someone does that they'd be considered weird."

To which we reply in the affirmative, alas. A strange world it is.

Celebrity: Rocker Richie Sambora to Denise Richards

Lovely Romantic Gift: $525 gold circle pendant

Comment: On the surface this gift appears rather innocuous and not particularly interesting. However, there is a catch: It was the same $525 gold circle pendant Sambora had given estranged wife Heather Locklear one year prior to that. Heather reportedly found the duplication "amusing"—but girlfriend Richards was perhaps not so amused.

Celebrity: David Beckham to wife Posh Spice

Lovely Romantic Gift: Platinum vibrator with a 10-carat diamond encrusted base, linked to a 16-carat diamond necklace—worth $1.8 million

Comment: According to our source, this platinum vibrator with diamond encrusted base is *one of only 10 in the whole, entire world.* We speculate that its rarity is due to poor demand—who in the world would want one? Probably only about 10 people. Plastic (presumably) works just as well, and you can use the millions you save to buy a yacht or a redwood tree house or a string of polo ponies or something more *practical.* News Flash: According to the vibrator designer and strip-club owner Peter Stringfellow, Mick Jagger, the aging rocker who has everything except a young you-know-what, has expressed interest in purchasing a platinum vibrator with diamond-encrusted base for his girlfriend L'Wren Scott.

Celebrity: Tom Cruise to then-gf and bearer of His Child Katie Holmes

Lovely Romantic Gift: DVD collection of every film he had been in, inscribed with a personal, handwritten love message to the then–future mother of the Child

Comment: What a wild, crazy, and *romantic* guy. The idea of a handwritten note introducing a DVD of *Top Gun* to one's love is simply over the top.

Celebrity: Ben Affleck to Jennifer Lopez

Lovely Romantic Gift: Toilet seat

Comment: But what a toilet seat! It was a *$105,000* toilet seat—encrusted with rubies, sapphires, pearls, and diamonds.

In Ben's words, Lopez's butt is "a famous thing. It should be treated well." He reportedly added that "Jennifer is my princess and she deserves only the best, even when it comes to toilets." One hopes that the diamonds were coated, otherwise they could have *scratched* the royal buttock cheeks.

What was J Lo's reaction to this quite distinctive gift designed to match her quite distinctive behind? Ben admitted, "It didn't go over that well."

Celebrity: Angelina Jolie to Brad Pitt
Lovely Romantic Gift: A dried bat in a small vial
Comment: Before anyone gets ideas, the dried bat was, naturally, for *safety's* sake: to keep in his glove compartment to ward off accidents.

Tips for a Perfect Celebrity-Style Wedding

After love, after the dried bats and the hot sex, comes marriage. Celebrities, being so rich and famous, represent *class.* They know how to do things with *style.* Like weddings. Here are some celebrity tips on making your wedding fabulous, fun, and classy—the celebrity way.

Tip #1: Say it with blood.

Blood. Not flowers. Flowers are so *passé.*

Angelina Jolie understands how blood makes a wedding *special.* Back in 1996, when the star married her *Hackers* costar Jonny Lee Miller, she wore black leather pants and a white shirt to the wedding. On the back of her white shirt she painted Miller's name in her own blood.

How utterly *romantic, non?*

"You're young, you're drunk, you're in bed, you have knives . . ." the actress once characteristically remarked. "Shit happens."

Tip #2: Make it a *toilet roll* wedding.

Toilet rolls make the wedding, they say.

They certainly did for Madonna. At her traditional wedding in December 2000 to Guy Ritchie, she was presented with a twin-pack of toilet paper by the Reverend Susan Brown, the minister who presided over the ceremony at the Church of Scotland cathedral in Dornoch, Scotland.

The good reverend explained the lovely and heart-warming significance of this perhaps not-so-traditional Scottish wedding gift:

"There are two rolls together just like the couple. And the toilet paper is soft, gentle, long and strong—which is what I hope their marriage will be."

Madonna really knows how to pick a number one reverend, or should we say a *number two*?

Tip #3: Can we talk wedding jeans, bikinis—and tattoos?

Maybe this is getting old. Pamela Anderson's *latest* wedding featured the buxom star in a (miniskirt) wedding "gown"—only afterward did she change into a classy wedding bikini with her new hubby's name on the butt. And a nice cute touch: Pam's "maid" of honor was photographer David LaChapelle! A guy!

How original.

But back in the old days, when Pamela married Tommy Lee, they were married on the beach with Pamela in a trademark white bikini and Tommy in shorts. No rings, of course. Instead, they had wedding rings tattooed on their fingers, along with each other's name.

Tip #4: Put dogs in your wedding.

Dogs certainly can add that indefinable something to your wedding. So why not a dog-human double wedding?

This utterly charming idea occurred to Tori Spelling and her husband, writer-actor Charlie Shanian. Tori and Charlie made their wedding a double one: They were joined by Tori's two dogs, Mimi and Leah, cutely dressed as a bride and groom—a pug in a white-veiled dress and a terrier in a little doggie tuxedo.

One question: Mimi and Leah are both the names of bitches (no comment on Tori); so was this a *gay* dog wedding? Legalistic types might want to note that gay weddings are still illegal in "enlightened" California.

Tip #5: Add that touch of surrealism to your wedding.

It may have been inadvertent, but we've got to say that Michael Douglas really knows how to make a wedding *memorable.*

He added that special surrealistic touch that truly added oomph.

On his website, he kindly offered fans a special sneak preview to his forthcoming wedding to Catherine Zeta-Jones. But he didn't stop there.

Let's let a fan who signed the site's special guest book tell us the rest of what happened: After his name was added to the list, "I started getting a stream of supposedly personalized e-mails from the actor himself."

Nice, but then not so nice . . .

Then, our Michael Douglas fan says, "Something at the site went terribly wrong." Literally *every* e-mail reply to an invitation to a special chat with Douglas was copied to *everyone* else on the website's mass-distribution list.

People were *deluged* with responses—from the fairly ordinary—"We'll be there with bells on!" (well, relatively ordinary)—to the quite bizarre—"My groins are not very good, but I am trying to improve it. I nevertheless hope to could greet you."

Now who could forget a wedding like that? Even if one's groins *were* good!

NECESSARY EXPENSES FOR A PROPER CELEBRITY WEDDING

Liza Minnelli and David Gest (divorced one year later) spent: $2.7 million

Some necessary accoutrements: Six-foot-tall cake, *Wizard of Oz* decorations

....

Paul McCartney and Heather Mills (separated four years later) spent: $3.2 million

Some necessary accoutrements: $1,500 white chocolate truffle cake, $150,000 worth of flowers, fireworks ($220,000), and gold-leaf plates for the 300 guests to eat off of

....

Donald Trump and Marla Maples (separated 4 years later) spent: approximately $1 million—relatively meager compared to many others

Some necessary accoutrements: $60,000 19-tier cake and $60,000 worth of Beluga caviar

....

Donald Trump and Melania Knauss (still married) spent: "millions"

Some necessary accoutrements: Custom-made wedding dress worth $100,000—with 13-foot train and even longer veil, $1.5 million ring for the bride (but the Donald only paid half price!), police escort

....

Melissa Rivers and John Endicott (divorced five years later) spent: nearly $2 million

Some necessary accoutrements: 30,000 white flowers, bride's initials handpainted on her Vera Wang gown

....

Beyoncé Knowles and Jay-Z spent: roughly $3 million

Some necessary accoutrements: $300,000 for Beluga caviar; lobster, Italian truffles, and Dom Pérignon; Oprah Winfrey and UN Secretary-General Kofi Annan among guests

Mercenary Marriages—or, Making Money the Old-Fashioned Way . . . Marrying It

Some marriages are for love, and some marriages are for, well, love also. It's just sheer luck that there's a little money involved too. Like ten million or so . . .

DIGGER	SUGAR SPOUSE	WHAT THEY GOT	WHAT THEY HAD TO DO	NOTES
Comedy writer turned comedian Tom Arnold	Roseanne	Some of Roseanne's money; acting roles including *True Lies* with Arnold Schwarzenegger; went on from there to host Fox Sports Net's talk show *Best Damn Sports Show Period* and do the voice for fast-food chain Arby's "Oven Mitt" TV commercial character	Have sex with Roseanne—which apparently wasn't fun for either of them, viz.: Roseanne: "Tom Arnold's penis is three inches long. Okay, I'll say four, 'cause we're trying to settle." Tom: "Even a 747 looks small when it lands in the Grand Canyon."	One of the lucky gold diggers who got a real career out of it (for some reason . . .), if one considers oven mitt voice-overs career material

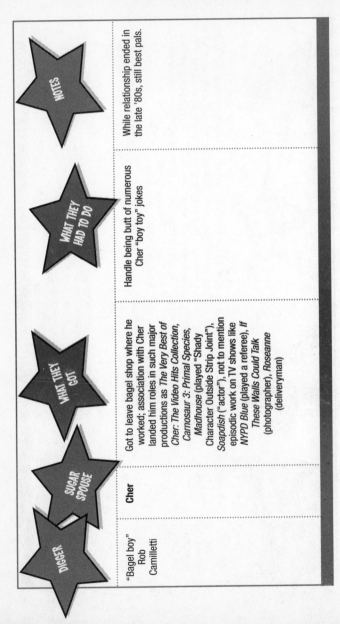

DIGGER	SUGAR SPOUSE	WHAT THEY GOT	WHAT THEY HAD TO DO	NOTES
"Bagel boy" Rob Camilletti	**Cher**	Got to leave bagel shop where he worked; association with Cher landed him roles in such major productions as *The Very Best of Cher: The Video Hits Collection*, *Carnosaur 3: Primal Species*, *Madhouse* (played "Shady Character Outside Strip Joint"), *Soapdish* ("actor"), not to mention episodic work on TV shows like *NYPD Blue* (played a referee), *If These Walls Could Talk* (photographer), *Roseanne* (deliveryman)	Handle being butt of numerous Cher "boy toy" jokes	While relationship ended in the late '80s, still best pals.

				Tried to sweeten prenup pot during divorce proceedings
Dancer Kevin Federline (aka K-Fed)	**Britney Spears**	Fledgling rap "career", access to Britney net worth	Dump pregnant girlfriend and impregnate Britney	Tried to sweeten prenup pot during divorce proceedings
Construction worker Larry Fortensky	**Elizabeth Taylor**	TV role—*The E! True Hollywood Story—Elizabeth Taylor* (1998) (played "Himself—Last Husband of Mrs. Taylor"); "hefty" chunk of money as part of divorce settlement	Marry her while not on drugs	Met at Betty Ford clinic, married at Michael Jackson's Neverland, divorced after five years
Actress Katie Holmes	**Tom Cruise**	Lots of press—but not necessarily of the right kind; a baby—but not necessarily . . . oh, never mind	Have sex (maybe) with Tom Cruise; start believing in Xenu; have Leah Remini and Jenna Elfman as BFFs	After giving birth, tried to revive career
Model Melania Knauss	**Donald Trump**	Access to Trump fortune; switched from modeling to burgeoning TV career. Credits include comic TV advertisement for Aflac insurance, in which she and the Aflac mascot, a duck, voiced by comedian Gilbert Gottfried, exchange personalities via a Frankenstein-like mad experiment. Also has appeared as a guest host on *The View*.	Have sex with Donald and his hair	Supposedly signed prenup, so money limited if/when they divorce (Marla Maples reportedly only got $2 mil)

DIGGER	SUGAR SPOUSE	WHAT THEY GOT	WHAT THEY HAD TO DO	NOTES
Actor Dean McDermott	Tori Spelling	Almost got access to Spelling fortune, but when Spelling dad died, inheritance money went pfft; tattoo on the wrist that reads "Truly Madly Deeply Tori"	Have sex with Tori Spelling	Plans to get tattoo of Tori's face on upper arm
Model Heather Mills	Paul McCartney	More face time in magazines	Pretend Paul was better than John; pretend Stella liked her	After separation, turned down $45 million, could get up to $200 million

Free(loading) Weddings

Weddings are expensive—for the rest of us, that is. Celebrities, if they so desire (and increasingly they do so desire), can get their wedding costs cut—or better yet, they can get *paid* to be married.

Particularly for the serial marriers, getting married not only can be an exciting way of defraying ballooning costs, it can be a lucrative *business*.

There are a number of ways to make the most romantic moment(s) of one's life even better by receiving that fat payoff in green dollar bills. Photographs can be sold, products can be plugged, freebies can be accepted, invitations can be offered for an appropriate honorarium. It's an increasingly common trend. Until recently, though, according to star wedding planner Mindy Weiss (who worked with Jessica Simpson), many celebrities avoided this "pay me" route—"because then they have to talk publicly about intimate parts of their lives" in return.

But nowadays, and particularly for your more basic "meat and potatoes" kind of celebrity (think reality show stars, runners-up on *American Idol*, Star Jones), it can be the best way to combine the two loves of a celebrity's life— a spouse and cold cash, not necessarily in that order.

Here are a few innovative as well as commonplace tips from stars on how you can defray wedding costs, beginning with the least expensive method.

Tip #1: Ask for freebies—like sweatsuits or chocolate.

Okay, we're not talking big money, but every little bit counts. And things like free sweatsuits for bridesmaids reduces costs (according to one Hollywood company which donates wedding sweatsuits, almost no Hollywood bride refuses them). Tori Spelling, whose father built one of the largest fortunes in Hollywood, accepted free chocolate candies for her wedding. Assuming one Godiva chocolate bar for each of the 300 guests, that's about $767 in savings. Not much, but then again, according to recent reports, Tori only got $800,000 from her father's estate. For some stars, just like the rest of us, every $100 has to count.

Tip #2: Televise your wedding!

Everyone and everything's on TV nowadays, why not your wedding? MTV paid the entire cost of Carmen Electra and Dave Navarro's (now unattached) wedding. *The Bachelorette*'s Trista Rehn and Ryan Sutter earned $1 million from ABC to air their 2003 wedding.

Tip #3: Sell the wedding photographs.

Depending on who you are, the tabloids might be interested in your wedding photographs. Catherine Zeta-Jones and Michael Douglas sold photo rights to their 2000 wedding for $1.4 million.

Cautionary note: Make sure you have the *exclusive* photographs. Zeta-Jones's wedding was scooped by *Hello!* magazine, which crashed the wedding and published its own photos. Zeta-Jones sued, only to have the press call her greedy for valuing her wedding photographs so highly.

Tip #4: Sell the rights to your wedding photographs, say you're donating the proceeds to charity—and then keep the money!

This kills two birds with one stone—you make money and you not only don't look like a money-grubbing greedhead for trying to make one of the most important days of your life a money-making proposition, you instead sound like a wonderful, caring person. Although they deny it, Demi Moore and Ashton Kutcher may have followed this innovative method. They were paid a cool $3 million for allowing *OK!* magazine exclusive access to their Beverly Hills wedding, and reports "suggested" that they were planning to donate the money to Habitat for Humanity. Habitat for Humanity denied getting any money, and when asked about the whole issue, Demi's publicist said somewhat lamely: "Demi wants to keep her charitable donations private and does not allow me to comment." Of course, it's possible that Moore and Kutcher have made numerous donations to Habitat since that denial was issued. But then, they keep their donations private, so who's to know?

Tip #5: Sell the ENTIRE wedding!

This is the pro level of making weddings pay. No namby-pamby hints of charitable contributions, just in-your-face capitalism with a capital C. Talk-show host and numero-uno Bridezilla Star Jones did it all when she married Al Reynolds. How? In two lovely words: corporate sponsorships.

She received donated invitations (Encore Studios and the Stationery Studio), tuxedos (Sarno & Son), and bridesmaids' gowns (Lazaro Bridal). There was even an official *airline* for the wedding (Continental). The groom was (reportedly) *not* donated. The bride star Star even provided on-air plugs for her wedding products on her show, *The View*, which was technically a no-no, but who was looking?

Till Death Do We Part (Well, Sort Of . . .): The Shortest Celebrity Marriages

Some celebrities sadly wind up with rather noxious nuptials—marriages that just don't *quite* make it.

In descending order, from the long-lived marriages—that is, those that almost made it to the one-year mark (amazing, but true!)—to those that lasted only a little longer than it took to say the vows.

LENGTH OF WEDDED BLISS	THE BLUSHING BRIDE	THE HAPPY GROOM	NOTES
8 months	Jennifer Lopez	Backup dancer Cris Judd	J Lo came out with the following: "Cris brings serenity into my world. In the midst of the crazy storm that is my life, his love is what I need most of all." Only a few weeks after she said this, it was all over—J Lo kept her cash; Cris got to keep their chocolate Labrador retriever named Buster.
7 months	Actress Renée Zellweger	Country singer Kenny Chesney	Married after meeting at a tsunami relief benefit 5 months earlier; ceremony took 15 minutes.
7 months	Actress Courtney Thorne-Smith	Scientist Andrew Conrad	Marriage was over one week before their wedding pictures appeared in In Style Weddings—with Courtney on the cover in her wedding dress.

LENGTH OF WEDDED BLISS	THE BLUSHING BRIDE	THE HAPPY GROOM	NOTES
5 months	Actress **Shannen Doherty**	"Actor" **Ashley Hamilton**	Knew each other for TWO WHOLE WEEKS before they married.
5 months	**Carmen Electra**	**Dennis Rodman**	Married after partying hard in Las Vegas; Rodman tried to get the marriage annulled after 9 (or 10) days, stating that he was so drunk he didn't even remember the ceremony and he didn't *mean* to get married . . . but, happily, they were able to work things out (for the next 4½ months . . . until Rodman was arrested for battery and they split for good).
5 months	**Drew Barrymore**	**Tom Green**	Very high profile in the 17 months before their marriage; divorced shortly after escaping a fire in their Bev Hills home. Green cutely commented: "I've had wind that lasted longer than our marriage."

LENGTH OF WEDDED BLISS	THE BLUSHING BRIDE	THE HAPPY GROOM	NOTES
4 months	Actress **Amelia Warner**	Actor **Colin Farrell**	Got married in private ceremony on Bora Bora—and, instead of wedding rings, had their names tattooed on their fingers; 4 months later when it came time to divorce things went swimmingly . . . since it turned out the marriage wasn't legal in the first place.
4 months, 24 days	**Donna Peele**	**Charlie Sheen**	Met 6 weeks before wedding; married a few weeks after Sheen testified at madam Heidi Fleiss's trial (he said he spent more than $50,000 in a year on her call girls); Sheen filed for divorce later, explaining, "There was a voice. Not like drug-induced voices, but there was a voice that kept telling me this will not work."

LENGTH OF WEDDED BLISS	THE BLUSHING BRIDE	THE HAPPY GROOM	NOTES
4 months	Actress **Pamela Anderson**	Singer **Kid Rock**	Explained the big-busted one: "I'm a spontaneous person. Maybe next time I'll think it through a little more."
3 months, 15 days	"Singer" **Lisa Marie Presley**	Actor (and major Elvis fan) **Nicolas Cage**	Rocky even before the actual wedding (Lisa Marie threw her massive diamond engagement ring into the ocean during one, um, spirited fight), but managed to pull it together to get married during the week of the 25th anniversary of Elvis's death. Sadly, the marriage died too—he filed for divorce and she said, "We shouldn't have got married in the first place."
1 month, 2 days	Belter **Ethel Merman**	Actor **Ernest Borgnine**	Let's just leave well enough alone on this one. We don't even want to imagine it. . . .

LENGTH OF WEDDED BLISS	THE BLUSHING BRIDE	THE HAPPY GROOM	NOTES
30 days (or 19 days, depending upon source)	**Drew Barrymore** (yes, again)	**Jeremy Thomas**	Knew each other 6 whole weeks; she (then 19) proposed to him in an alley; were married by a minister they found in the Yellow Pages. Drew said, "I'm so lucky to have met this person" —before they divorced, of course.
14 days	Actress/model **Ali Landry**	Actor **Mario López**	Dated for 6 years; finally got married—but only 3 days after the wedding, Lopez reportedly started partying with other women.
9 days	*Dynasty* actress and actual princess **Catherine Oxenberg**	Producer **Robert Evans**	Married 4 days after they met; Evans (then 68) had recently almost died— which gave him the perfect reason for the annulment: "I forgot it had only been six weeks since I had been hit with a stroke."

LENGTH OF WEDDED BLISS	THE BLUSHING BRIDE	THE HAPPY GROOM	NOTES
9 days	**Cher**	Musician **Gregg Allman**	3 days after Cher divorced Sonny, the couple flew to Vegas to marry. Shortly thereafter, Cher was shocked, *shocked*, to discover that Gregg had too many drug and alcohol problems . . . and filed for divorce.
8 days	Singer **"Mama" Michelle Phillips**	Actor **Dennis Hopper**	Married on Halloween; Hopper later said the whole thing was a bit of a blur since he had been doing a lot of drugs and alcohol.
55 hours	**Britney Spears**	Hometown pal **Jason Alexander** (not the *Seinfeld* one)	Another Vegas do; the bride wore jeans and a baseball cap and was walked down the aisle by a hotel bellman; later claimed it was all just a funny spur-of-the-moment jokey kinda thing. . . .

10

CELEBRITY PREGNANCY AND CHILDREN

AN INEVITABLE OFFSHOOT OF being a celebrity is having sex. And celebrity sex, as we know, produces pregnant celebrity women and, ultimately, celebrity children. As one may imagine, this produces many opportunities for celebrities to be unusually annoying, stupid, or otherwise exasperatingly tedious. To say nothing of their spawn . . .

The Preggo Awards: In Honor of Truly Inspired Celebrity Pregnancy Moments

Celebrities get pregnant. It's one of those facts that helps sell so many tabloids. And when they get *enceinte* as the old gossip columns used to put it, they go through just *so much*! As if it's not difficult enough dealing with a basic pregnancy, stars have to also manage being, well, stars. But also *good parent-to-be* stars, dammit!

To put it bluntly, they impress the hell out of us. Truly they do. And we want to reward them. We want everyone to realize just how incredibly marvelous and just so goldurn amazing they are for being stars AND dealing with pregnancy as well in ways that we norms just would never imagine.

(Let's take a pause so we can all wipe away a tear. Those freakin' hormones are getting us all weirded out. . . . Oh, wait—maybe we should try Scientology? Never mind. . . .)

Now that we're all composed . . . let us confer the Preggos on those celebrities who really have gone above and beyond the norm when it comes to being pregnant.

The "I'm a Supportive Husband to My Pregnant Wife" Award goes to . . . Donald Trump

. . . who, understanding that hormonal fluctuations can make a mom-to-be a tad weepy at times and that her changing body can make a mom-to-be a little more hyper than usual about her self-image, took great care to be sensitive and caring.

A prime example of this sensitivity: The proud papa-to-be couldn't help bragging about wife Melania on the Howard Stern radio show—where, to a huge listening audience, he sweetly commented:

> "She really has become a monster. . . . I mean 'monster' in the most positive way."

Aww . . .

The "Avoiding Toxicity Prenatal Dietary Excellence" Award goes to . . . Britney Spears

. . . who made sure she ate only the right foods while pregnant with her first child, Sean Preston.

Yes, Brit was a careful mother-to-be. And we're not only talking about taking her prenatal vitamins. We're talking about avoiding anything that could harm the baby. You know, like that scourge of a successful pregnancy. Ominous Frito chips.

Case in point: When Britney was in a Malibu supermarket with her sister Jamie, she suddenly noticed the Frito she was eating. "Everything is wrong! Look at this Frito . . . it's shaped like a TWO-HEADED BABY! This is a sign . . . an omen!" "You're creeping me out," Jamie reportedly said. So Britney did what any concerned mother-to-be would do: She stomped on the chip and said she would eat no more Fritos until the baby was born.

The "Planning Ahead Award" goes to . . . Madonna

. . . who made *sure* her baby was born on the right day.

When pregnant with daughter Lourdes, Madonna was told by her spiritual mentor that the most auspicious time for the baby to be born would be during a new moon. Madonna—a take-charge type if we ever saw one—didn't want to take any chances. She reportedly scheduled a C-section for a new moon day.

The Boy Scout "Be Prepared" Award goes to . . . Tom Cruise

. . . who, wanting to be sure that all went hunky dory when then-fiancée Katie "She Who Is to Be Called Kate" Holmes was preggers, laid in all the necessary equipment at home.

Not just diaper bags and baby binkies, but an ultrasound machine, fetal monitor, intravenous pump, delivery kit, and infant warmer system. (Oh, and three Scientology medics, a midwife, a nurse, and an obstetrics expert too, natch.) Luckily for Katie, though, reports of a large adult-sized pacifier to be used by the mother were rumors.

The "What We Don't See Can't Hurt Us" Award goes to . . . Angelina Jolie and Brad Pitt

. . . who made sure the birth of their first biological child was a very private affair (even if a few people had to be threatened, such a shame . . .).

Angelina and Brad were in Namibia anticipating the birth of their child—and worried about the frenzied attention of reporters and photographers. What to do? Why, hire a top-notch security guy, of course! Who could close roads and hire a top-notch security team—a team allegedly made up of members of an apartheid counterinsurgency unit, of course! A top-notch security team that would chase local kids off public beaches near Angie and Brad's place, that would threaten press members hoping to get a story, and that would generally not make nice-nice with anyone vaguely within the vicinity of the stars.

One Namibian resident summed it all up: "I sympathize with Brad Pitt and Angelina because they do want privacy, but on the other hand they are public figures and there is a lot of interest in their visit. From what I hear they are nice people but their security guys most certainly aren't."

The "I'm Ready for My Close-up, Mr. DeMille" Award goes to . . . Demi Moore

. . . who made absolutely sure that the marvelous moment of childbirth would be captured from moment one.

But unlike most people who have the nervous father using a videocam, Demi the perfectionist hired three cameramen to film the birth of her first baby. As she was pushing, pushing, pushing—and the baby's head began to show—Moore yelled, "Are you guys getting this?"

A MODEL PREGNANCY

When supermodel Cindy Crawford was in the first months of her pregnancy, she had a teeny tiny bump—not much bigger than her much-vaunted mole—and some very fascinating words on the whole idea of, like, pregnancy:

> "You don't even look pregnant, which is weird 'cause you are pregnant, but you don't look pregnant."

Fun Celebrity Placenta Tricks

Ever think to yourself, "What in the world will I do with this pesky placenta now that I/my partner have/has given birth?"

Think no more! Celebrities, of course, have some really GREAT ideas!

(You may want to take notes. . . .)

Placenta Idea #1: Bury placenta in backyard during moving family ceremony.

Rod Stewart and wife Penny think this is a great way of welcoming the new baby—and it's a family bonding experience to boot! Cleverly planning ahead, they froze the placenta until Rod's children could come to England from L.A. Then they thawed it, drenched the placenta in tea tree oil and put it in a hole they had dug in their garden.

Says Penny: "I said a few words like, 'This is for our little Alastair. May he have a long and healthy life.' Rod passed a spade to Liam, who shoveled in some earth. Then we all took turns. We all jumped on the top and flattened the ground. It was a resting place for it." And such a lovely memory. (We are not sure of its effects on soil—positive or negative.)

Placenta Idea #2: Eat placenta for nutritive purposes.

Tom Cruise told *GQ*, "I'm going to eat the placenta. I thought that would be very good. I'm going to eat the cord and the placenta right there."

And why the heck not? It supported the baby's life, so it must be chock-full of vitamins and minerals, right? But Tom later told Diane Sawyer on *Good Morning America* that it was all a funny joke intended to make light of all the rumors floating around about his baby (not to mention his "relationship" with Katie Holmes): "Yeah, we're going to do that—a whole family thing. Isn't that normal and natural. No, we're not eating it." Tom, you're such a kidder!

Placenta Idea #3: Eat placenta for beauty purposes.

Singapore actress Cassandra See *wasn't* kidding about eating her placenta. After giving birth to her son, she roasted the placenta in the oven until it was dry and crisp. She then pounded it into a powder and poured it into capsules—which she took every morning before eating. She claims her placenta pills not only helped her recover from the C-section, but also gave her a "glowing complexion."

Placenta Idea #4: DON'T eat placenta (but keep in fridge until koi pond is ready).

Pamela Anderson apparently isn't in the "let's all chow down on placenta" bandwagon. But she *did* keep it in her fridge. She was careful, though, to make sure it wouldn't wind up as part of someone's midnight nosh—and labeled the bag DO NOT EAT. She told *Men's Fitness*, "We're going to put it in our koi pond once our yard is finished."

Fascinating Facts About Post-Pregnancy Bods from the Mouths of Stars

Trust a celebrity mom to share the glories and wonders of her pregnancy with the rest of the world. Aren't we *lucky* to learn the following? (Hmm. Maybe not . . .)

"It's strange getting this, because my mind is on my baby and my breasts—which are ready to unload any second."

> —KATE HUDSON, accepting an award from *Premiere* magazine

"My stomach is all crinkly and my boobs, they're like the ears of a dog."

> —KATE WINSLET, explaining what happened after she had two kids

"When I got through with the twin pregnancy, my abdominal skin was such that I had to fold it up and then stick it in my pants."

> —CYBILL SHEPHERD

"I thought *National Geographic* boobs only happened in the magazine. It wasn't until after I had the baby, I went, 'Oh, no!' And . . . every morning with the bra, you have to do 'the scoop' . . . That's what it's come to."

> —JENNY MCCARTHY

And the good news? You *can* lose that pesky pregnancy weight! As Kate Winslet, once again being as candid as can be, tells us: "My bottom no longer looks like a purple sprouting broccoli."

Being a Good Parent, Celebrity-Style

Parenting is tough. Everyone knows that. So aren't we lucky that we have celebrities to emulate? Talk about having enlightened parenting skills! We all could learn from them. To that end, then, here are just a few tips from some truly amazing celebrity parents:

Celebrity Parenting Tip #1: Childproof your house—cover electrical outlets, put locks on cabinets, get rid of pet sharks.

Britney Spears is the picture-perfect "safety first" kind of mom. While pregnant with her second child, she made an important decision: then-hub Kevin Federline had to get rid of his six pet sharks. Britney got a little worried that the Australian gray nurse sharks might not be family-friendly when there were *two* children in the family. (Apparently, it was fine and dandy having sharks when there was only *one* child. Two? A different story.) So even though Kevin adores his toothy pets (he even named them), the sharks have to go in deference to the mommy-to-be's wishes.

Celebrity Parenting Tip #2: Commemorate those special occasions by showing meaningful, special, family videos.

This sounds like the type of thing many parents do. But Sting and wife Trudie Styler upped the stakes a bit by showing a very special video to all the guests at his son's large 21st birthday bash. One guest explained: "Everyone was expecting a video of Jake as a kid, when this pretty gruesome film of his birth started." And it was a *detailed* video of his birth—complete with Trudie push, push, pushing, head emerging from vagina . . . the whole nine yards. Said Trudie: "Jake's a film producer now so I thought it would be a good idea to show his first film role. I think it was all quite sweet." Sweet, maybe. Graphic, definitely.

Celebrity Parenting Tip #3: Don't get so lost in your parenting role that you forget your *own* needs.

Celebrity parents know it's all too easy to be so engrossed in being a mom or dad that you lose sight of yourself as an individual. A sexual individual at that. So they make sure that they remember to take care of themselves—and to let their children know about it. And don't mince words!

For example, Courtney Love was up-front and honest with her sixth-grade daughter Frances Bean. Talking about an upcoming event, she said, "Maybe I'll meet Jack White, and he'll be my new boyfriend. Mommies need to get laid, too."

Celebrity Parenting Tip #4: For that matter, don't be afraid to make choices based on yourself as an individual, not as a parent.

Ryan O'Neal was equally open with his 16-year-old daughter Tatum O'Neal when he first started dating Farrah Fawcett. As he explained, "I had to make this choice between Tatum and this girl—and I chose Farrah. Tatum made me choose. I said, 'That's a bad idea. I sleep with this girl, Tatum. I don't sleep with you.'"

Thank heavens for that, at least!

Celebrity Parenting Tip #5: Set reasonable family rules to keep things running smoothly.

Madonna knows how to do this. She has nice simple rules that the kids have to follow and she's very explicit about them. No TV. No magazines. No milk. No ice cream. In addition to reasonable rules, she has set reasonable punishments for major infractions—like leaving clothes on the floor. "We take all of her [Lourdes's] clothes and put them in a bag and she has to earn all of her clothes back by being tidy. She wears the same outfit every day to school until she learns her lesson."

Celebrity Parenting Tip #6: Be REALLY strict when necessary.

Don't be a patsy! Let the kids know who's boss! Arnold Schwarzenegger is no pushover—like Madonna, he's strict about things . . . like laundry. If his kids leave their clothes lying around, he burns them. Yes. Burns them. In fire. (Wait! Not the kids. The clothes. He's not *that* strict.) Actually, in fairness to the Governator, he doesn't *always* burn them—he sometimes just takes the clothes and doesn't give them back. Even Ahnold has a soft side. . . .

Celebrity Parenting Tip #7: Teach your child about "hate language"—and ban certain hurtful words that only exist to demean others. Like . . . "fat"?

It's never too early to let kids know that certain words should never *ever* be used. That's why super-skinny Sarah Jessica Parker has already laid down the law to her toddler. He cannot use the word "fat." As she explained, "I've forbidden the word 'fat' because I don't like the way it's used and I don't want him to ever use that word." A laudable, if somewhat . . . excessive . . . notion.

Celebrity Parenting Tip #8: Give your child the joy of being able to help you . . . however.

Michael Douglas was stung by a jellyfish while vacationing in Majorca—and decided to try an old folk remedy. More specifically, he asked his six-year-old son Dylan to "pee-pee on Daddy's back." According to Daddy Douglas, his son "looked at me like he'd gone to heaven. I don't know if it helped at all, but my son was happy." Now isn't that a precious picture?

Beyond "Apple": The Most Ridiculous Celebrity Children Names

Many celebrities seem a tad hung up on the idea of being different, being creative, and generally being oh-so-unique-and-clever. This isn't a bad thing in and of itself, but it gets a little more worky when it extends to their children.

In other words, a lot of celebrities go more than a little bonkers when they name their kids. Gwyneth Paltrow got a lot of press when she and rocker hub Chris Martin named their little girl "Apple." But "Apple" is almost *bland* compared to other celebrity offspring names.

Read 'em and weep . . . or laugh . . . or puke.

WHEN A COOL-SOUNDING NAME GOES A LITTLE BAD— OR, SORRY, SURI!

Tom Cruise and Katie Holmes thought they had a great name choice for their daughter: Suri. "It means 'princess' in Hebrew," a family spokesperson explained of their choice.

Well . . . problem is, Suri *doesn't* mean "princess" in Hebrew. Not according to a bunch of Hebrew language experts.

In Hebrew, Suri *does* mean "a person from Syria," or "Get out of here" . . . or, more colloquially, "Scram!"

Maybe they were thinking of the *other* meanings of Suri in other languages? Well . . . maybe not. Suri, in other languages, is a Nubian tribe, a Hindi boy's name, and a term for a form of alpaca's wool. Oh, and it also means "pickpocket" in Japanese and "pointy nose" in some Indian dialects.

OH-SO-UNIQUE CELEBRITY CHILD NAME	CELEB PARENT(S) WHO BESTOWED THIS NAME
Audio Science (boy)	Actress **Shannyn Sossamon**
Aurelius Cy (boy)	Model **Elle MacPherson**
Banjo (boy)	Actress **Rachel Griffiths**
Bluebell Madonna (girl)	**Geri Halliwell**
Diezel (boy)	Singer **Toni Braxton**
Denim (boy)	**Toni Braxton**
Elijah Bob Patricius Guggi Q (boy)	**Bono**
Heavenly Hiraani Tiger Lilly (girl)	Singer **Michael Hutchence** and TV personality **Paula Yates**
Henry Gunther Ademola Dashtu Samuel (boy)	Model **Heidi Klum** and singer **Seal**
Kal-el (boy)	**Nicolas Cage**
Moxie CrimeFighter (girl)	Comedian **Penn Jillette**
Peaches Honeyblossom Michelle Charlotte Angel Vanessa (girl)	Singer **Bob Geldof** and TV personality **Paula Yates**
Pilot Inspektor (boy)	Actor **Jason Lee**
Speck Wildhorse (boy)	Singer **John Mellencamp**

ON THE POOR KID

Note: Peaches Geldof is speaking out for the other celebrity kids with insano monikers, begging parents to think before they slap a stupid name on their child: "I hate ridiculous names, my weird name has haunted me all my life."

Baby Bling—or, How to Raise a Child on Only $2 Million a Year

Celebrity babies require celebrity accoutrements—rather costly ones, at that. But anyone on a strict budget of say, $2 or so million can happily follow the stars and indulge Baby.

A few suggestions:

ITEM	ITEM PRICE	CELEB PARENT	COMMENTS
Monogrammed burp cloths	$37 for three	Rosie O'Donnell, Sharon Stone, Julia Louis-Dreyfus	Let Baby throw up and drool with class!
Chinese silk receiving blankets	$56 each	Lisa Kudrow, Catherine Keener	Get Baby used to silk instead of that nasty common fleece or cotton!
Gucci diaper bag	$865	Jada Pinkett Smith	Prada is also acceptable.

ITEM	ITEM PRICE	CELEB PARENT	COMMENTS
Chandelier for nursery	$1,200	**Britney Spears**	Luxury light fixtures are essential for someone who spends much time lying on back staring at ceiling.
Titanium stroller	$2,000	**Jerry Seinfeld, Madonna, Catherine Zeta-Jones**	The Jaguar drivers of tomorrow demand Martinelli titanium wheels today!
Diamond stud earrings (for baby girl)	$4,300	**Gwyneth Paltrow**	What every 17-month toddler is wearing!
Diamond stud earrings	$47,500	**Victoria "Posh" Beckham**	They match daddy's!
Playhouse	$85,000	**Demi Moore**	Mini-mansion includes full bath, air-conditioning, and furniture. Price was high, but, hey, real estate ain't cheap!

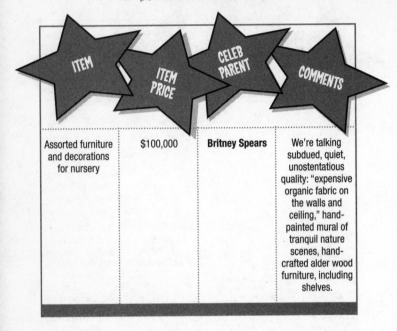

ITEM	ITEM PRICE	CELEB PARENT	COMMENTS
Assorted furniture and decorations for nursery	$100,000	**Britney Spears**	We're talking subdued, quiet, unostentatious quality: "expensive organic fabric on the walls and ceiling," hand-painted mural of tranquil nature scenes, hand-crafted alder wood furniture, including shelves.

Baby's First Christmas

If you want to make sure your child has the best Christmas ever, one he or she will remember for years—perhaps with a touch of fear or even sheer horror à la *House of Wax*—take a hint from Britney:

For Sean Preston's first Christmas, she reportedly turned his room into a LIFE-SIZE nativity setting. With six LIFE-SIZE waxwork models of the important people involved, LIFE-SIZE donkeys, and LIFE-SIZE cattle. The proud mom selected Sean Preston to play the part of Baby Jesus—supplying a charming cherrywood manger for verisimilitude.

11

CELEBRITY HOMES

ONE OF THE FIRST things a celebrity does when he or she becomes a celebrity is to buy a home—usually with grotesque excesses that mark the true nouveau riche.

Think Versailles . . . but not with a cut-rate King of France budget.

What Every Celebrity Home Really Needs

So you want to live like a celebrity? You must, then, be sure you have those little accoutrements in your home that show you can keep up with the Joneses (and the Dions and the Afflecks, etc. etc.)

A few suggestions of things you should add to your home if you want that celebrity lifestyle:

Soccer Field

(Note: We'll make a concession here and say that you can also build a baseball diamond or football gridiron, depending upon your preference.)

Cost: $100,000

Rod Stewart, a rabid fan of the Celtic FC, had a soccer field—complete with dressing rooms just like his favorite team's—built on the grounds of his Epping, England, mansion.

Super-duper Garages

Cost: $2 million

Where to put all those expensive cars? Why, in an expensive garage, of course! Jay Leno had special garages built to house his 160 vintage cars. (No word on where he parks his plain ol' Dodge. . . .) And Jerry Seinfeld spent a relatively cheap $880,000 for a two-story building next to his apartment to use as a garage. Granted, he also had to shell out another $500k for a gut renovation, but wasn't it really worth it? Sadly, though, the garage will only hold about 20 cars.

300-Square-Foot Closet—For Shoes

Cost: $200,000

Singer Celine Dion knows how difficult it is to have enough closet space. So—faced with over 1,000 pairs of shoes, she did what any right-minded celebrity would do: coughed up $200,000 to have a closet custom-built just for her shoes.

Bowling Alley (Eight Lanes)

A logical addition to one's home, especially if one happens to have said home on a private Pacific island in northern Fiji. (Doesn't *everyone* own an island?) Like Mel Gibson. He bought a bowling alley—the first and only bowling alley in Fiji—from its owner after it went out of business, and had the alley shipped to his private island, Mago (which he had spent about $15 million for).

Attached Dwelling . . . for Doll Collection

Cost: $500,000

Just think—it's kind of like a "mother-in-law" addition, but without the mother-in-law! Demi Moore is the one we have to thank for this brilliant idea. Way back when she was still hooked up with Bruce Willis, she spent $500,000 for a house attached to her place in Idaho—just to house her doll collection.

Landing Strip—and Jumbo Jets

Cost: N/A—presumably in the millions

It's not enough to own a house or five. To truly attain the lifestyles of the rich and famous, you also need jets (three—jumbo ones). And, if you've got the jets, you need landing strips, n'est-ce pas? Just like John Travolta—who has landing strips built by each of his five houses . . . perfect for landing one of his three jumbo jets!

Waterfall in Bedroom

You can bring nature indoors—even if you live in an urban area like, say, rapper Ludacris. He has a nice waterfall right in the master bedroom. The only problem? We suggest you might also want a bathroom close by just in case the sound of the water gets things going. . . .

Enough Bathrooms (Like, Say, Oh, Something Like 38) and Enough TV Sets in the Master Bedroom (Five)

Mike Tyson didn't often use this particular house in Connecticut (he owned five others), but he made sure that he would never be caught waiting for the bathroom—there were 38 in the house. And, to make sure he could always catch whatever he wanted on TV, he had five TVs in his bedroom.

Appropriate Decorations—Like, Say, a Woman's Reproductive System

Jane Fonda loves how she designed the entryway into her apartment: an atrium painted pale pink with large silver doors leading out. "I designed it myself," she told a reporter. "It represents the womb. The doors are the labia and this [the hall] is the birth canal." How utterly *charming*!

One Is Never Enough: A Celebrity House Scorecard

"The more, the better" is the motto of many celebs when it comes to home ownership. A few notable multi-home-owning stars:

Elton John (an estate in Windsor, England, a condo in Atlanta, a high-rise in London, and a house in Nice, France)

Jack Osbourne (mom Sharon says he rents three of them out for rental income)

4 HOMES

John Travolta (who also owns 3 jumbo jets)

5 HOMES

Martha Stewart (5 houses, one New York City condo)

6 HOMES

Sting (including a 60-acre estate in Salisbury, England, a $6 million Malibu beach house, and a 240-hectare estate in Tuscany. He said: "We make use of the houses, it's not as if they lie fallow.")

7 HOMES

Catherine Zeta-Jones and Michael Douglas (including two mansions in Los Angeles, a New York apartment, a ski home in Colorado, a villa in Majorca, a house in Catherine's Welsh hometown of Mumbles, a house they are building in Canada, and a family home in Bermuda)

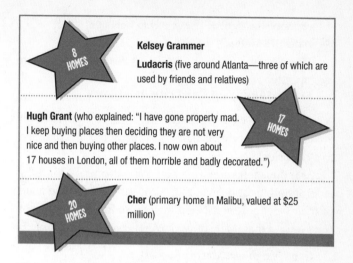

8 HOMES

Kelsey Grammer

Ludacris (five around Atlanta—three of which are used by friends and relatives)

Hugh Grant (who explained: "I have gone property mad. I keep buying places then deciding they are not very nice and then buying other places. I now own about 17 houses in London, all of them horrible and badly decorated.")

17 HOMES

20 HOMES

Cher (primary home in Malibu, valued at $25 million)

The Flip Side: Stars Who Want *Less*

Of course, then there are those stars who feel that you *can* have too much of a good thing, even when it comes to houses. Two simple down-to-earth celebrities immediately come to mind:

Barbra Streisand—avid environmentalist and simple gal from Brooklyn—explained: "I only want two houses rather than seven. I feel like letting go of things." Of course, one of her houses is a 10,000-square-foot oceanfront mansion in Malibu . . . but it's the thought that counts. Right?

Jennifer Lopez wasn't crazy about her Hollywood house because it was too much of a "movie star house." She wanted something more cozy, more *intime.* So she sold the Hollywood place and bought a new place on Long Island. "It was a movie star house. I've bought a smaller one instead. We have a house in Long Island like a French château.

It's glamorous but still homely." Yup, châteaus are just perfect when you want to downsize. . . .

Annoying Celebrity Neighbors

"Good fences make good neighbors," wrote the poet Robert Frost. All we can think is that clearly ol' Bob didn't live next to a celebrity.

As if these folks aren't already doing their most for us by entertaining us and such, they also contribute to the good of their neighborhoods! And they do so in a wide range of ways—ways that many of us may never have thought of.

Good Neighbor: Martha Stewart
Neighborly Activity: Filing lawsuit against neighbor to keep out ghastly "inappropriate dark greenery"

Martha is, of course, very attuned to the aesthetic nature of her neighborhood and, dadgummit, she wants to preserve it. So imagine her horror and, indeed, disgust when she noticed that her East Hampton neighbor, Harry Macklowe, had planted *shrubbery* between their two houses. Yes, shrubbery.

Gasp.

Martha quickly contacted the village zoning board, explaining that obviously Macklowe was trying to "suburbanize the area with inappropriate dark greenery." The board ruled that the shrubs had been planted illegally, and she was given the green light to remove the shrubs. But that was just the beginning. . . . Stewart and Macklowe embarked upon a years-long feud—all via the lucky city council—which ended up with a pile of paperwork concerning the various disputes that, while shorter than the inappropriate shrubbery, was still pretty high: one foot.

Good Neighbor: Martha Stewart

Neighborly Activity: Ridding neighborhood of offensive fence by pinning neighbor's landscaper to gate with car

In this case, it was Martha's neighbor's landscaper that got caught in the crossfire—or, more rightly, on the bumper. Macklowe was building a *fence* between their two houses. Yes, fence. A fence that would PARTIALLY BLOCK MARTHA'S VIEW OF THE POND!

Gasp.

Martha came home to find the workmen hard at work building said fence and expressed her disapproval in a robust and earthy manner. According to public records, she called one of the men working on the fence, Matthew Munnich, Macklowe's landscaper, a few robust and earthy names, then pinned him against a security gate control box with her Suburban. Munnich, a bit miffed, filed a criminal case against her for harm inflicted. The court declined to press charges, telling Munnich to take it up in civil court instead—which he did. Martha, no pushover, denied any wrongdoing and sued *him* for defamation, claiming he and his lawyer were using the story to extort money and that they had damaged her "international reputation for graciousness, rectitude, honesty and thriftiness." Her case was tossed. His case was settled out of court.

Good Neighbor: Sean Penn

Neighborly Activity: Perfuming neighborhood with stink from the aluminum Airstream trailer he lives in

Sean Penn is a natural kinda guy. And he has a natural kinda trailer on his 20-acre hillside plot.

"Natural" in this case means "smelly."

Yes, Penn's aluminum Airstream trailer stinks, reeks, and generally emits an offensive odor. He first moved into it in 1993 after his house was destroyed in a fire and apparently still loves the trailer lifestyle. But there's that stench. . . . One neighbor summed it up by saying, "He does not appear to have adequate drainage. It annoys us. And it can't be fun living in there when it's 100°F outside." It also can't be fun living near it. Penn, however, has made no comment on his neighbors' complaints.

Good Neighbor: Prince
Neighborly Activity: Beautifying neighborhood by painting house with tasteful bright purple stripes

Maybe Prince thought his neighbors would love his unique color scheme. But one thing is certain: His landlord, NBA star Carlos Boozer, didn't. When Prince rented a mansion, he "customized" the house by painting it with purple stripes (his fave color) and his Prince "symbol"—this design that he says is his name. He also painted "3121"—the title of his then-current album—on the house. His landlord filed suit against him, but Prince's lawyers countered by saying that Boozer had been collecting all the rent checks without any complaints about Prince's renovations. The lawsuit was withdrawn.

Good Neighbor: Matthew McConaughey
Neighborly Activity: Entertaining neighborhood with loud impromptu nude bongo playing . . . at 3 A.M.

Talk about your fun neighbors! Why sleep when you can listen to bongo playing in the nude in the early morning?

This is, of course, a rhetorical question since we'd venture to guess that many of us would prefer *not* to listen to nude bongos at 3 A.M. One of Matthew McConaughey's neighbors certainly felt that way—calling the police to complain about loud noise. When the police arrived at McConaughey's house an officer looked in the window, saw the actor dancing around nude and playing the bongos while another man clapped. When the officer opened the door, there was a distinct aroma of marijuana. The officer then decided to search the place and found a bowl filled with pot stems and seeds, a bong and a pipe. According to the police report, the two men had "glassy and very blood-shot eyes" and appeared "very intoxicated." McConaughey was arrested on charges of drug possession (which were dropped due to lack of evidence) and "resisting transportation" (he had to be forced into the squad car). (The drug charges were dropped; he pleaded guilty to violating Austin's noise ordinance and paid a $50 fine.)

Good Neighbor: Eva Longoria

Neighborly Activity: Making sure neighbors don't miss the lovely early morning hours by waking them up at 5:30 A.M. via beating a gong

Eva finds the early morning to be an energizing and beautiful time—and she apparently wants her Hollywood Hills neighbors to share her appreciation. So every morning at about 5:30 A.M. she hits a gong. (Not bong. She is no Matthew McConaughey.) *Star* magazine quoted one "bleary-eyed local" as saying, "Her morning ritual involves striking a gong several times." We do not know what she does after gong-striking, but we have a feeling we know what her neighbors do. (Hint: It involves strong language.)

Good Neighbor: Alyssa Milano

Neighborly Activity: Gardening au naturel

Alyssa Milano loves nature—to such a degree that she prefers to garden sans shirt, bra, or other top covering. "I garden topless. I'll be in my garden, you know, just being natural," she explained. Interestingly, no neighbors have complained.

12

THE SPIRITUAL CELEBRITY

AFTER READING ABOUT REAL estate (see prior chapter), the mind naturally turns to theological questions: Is there a God? If so, why has he created such a volatile real estate market? Will studying the Kabbalah reduce my mortgage costs? And where does the afterlife fit into this?

Celebrities also ask questions like this—or so we've heard.

Theories of God as Elucidated by Celebrities

As we've said, celebrities often ponder the basic big questions, like is there a God? And, if so, who (or what) is He (or She)? Like Thomas Aquinas or Maimonides—celebrities of a sort in their time—modern celebrities cum theologians have some fascinating, indeed insightful, theories.

The Traditional God (according to theologian/singer Britney Spears): Your basic time-honored theory, very prevalent among people up to age 8 . . . or perhaps 10.

"[In heaven] everyone is at peace and happy and they all hop around from cloud to cloud. . . . And an old man with a long, white beard wanders around—that's God."

The Mystical God (courtesy of theologian/actor David Arquette): God is a force, and He might look like a dildo.

"I think God is a giant vibrator in the sky . . . a pulsating force of incredible energy."

The Really Totally Neat God (courtesy of theologian/actress Justine Bateman): God is just too rad to describe coherently. Like, OMFG, you know?

"[God's] like, so cool. Think of the coolest person in your life. He made that person. And *He's* cooler than *that*."

The Career-Planning God (courtesy theologian/disco singer Donna Summer): Like a good headhunter, God will pull strings to make sure you get the right job.

"God had to create disco music so that I could be born and be successful."

The Rewarding God (courtesy of theologian/socialite/ "singer" Paris Hilton): God is a sugar daddy. And if your life sucks, it's your fault.

"I have good karma. . . . I am a good person, so God made things happen for me."

The High-Living God (courtesy of theologian/rapper Mase): God is a successful homey who likes grills, nice rims, and (probably) Courvoisier, but not Cristal.

"He don't have no problem with you blinging. God's heavenly abode proves that he is the real king of bling. His gates are pearly, his house is about 10 stadiums big, the streets are gold. You do the budget on that kind of place."

The "Appearances Matter" God (courtesy of theologian/rapper Mary J. Blige): God wants you to max out your credit card and look great.

"My God is a God who wants me to have things. He wants me to bling. He wants me to be the hottest thing on the block. I don't know what kind of God the rest of y'all are serving, but the God I serve says, 'Mary, you need to be the hottest thing this year, and I'm gonna make sure you're doing that.' My God's the bomb!"

Damn Spiritual Celebrities

Celebrities are, if they say so themselves, pretty damn deep and spiritual. They prove it in myriad ways—in the way they live (deeply and spiritually), in the things they appreciate (deep and spiritual), in the activities they engage in (deep and spiritual), and in the way they think (yes, deeply and spiritually).

Perhaps we can all pick up some hints about how to live a more deep and spiritual life by looking at what celebrities do. Then again, perhaps not. . . . You be the judge.

Jerry Hall's Hair Is Negativity-free! (Thanks to Feng Shui)

Have you ever wondered about model/former Mick Jagger gal Jerry Hall's hair? More specifically, have you wondered how in the world she keeps those long blond tresses from being negative? Wonder no more! She goes to a salon in Dallas and gets her hair feng shui-ed, naturally. Yes. Feng shui, as in moving furniture around your house to the "relationship" or the "fortune" quadrant (which is all based upon the notion that there's this big dragon living inside the earth, but no one bothers talking about that part these days . . .). "I go to this guy and he just gets all the negativity out," Jerry explains. "This guy" has the spiritual name of "Michael Motorcycle."

India.Arie's Birthday Is Only a *DAY AFTER GANDHI'S*! (Which Is Why She Is the Way She Is)

Singer India.Arie knows why she's such an enlightened, politically aware person. It's all in her name—and in her birthday. "The truth about my name is that . . . I believe people *choose* their names and that our names say a lot about what our destiny in life is." Umm . . . okay. But, wait. There's more and it's even *more* fascinating: "I discovered that my birthday was October 3rd and Mahatma Gandhi was October 2nd. But when I discovered it, I *knew* there was something to it. Once I started making music I started to understand that the political statements I make in my music and doing it in an honest but non-offensive way said a lot about his character and the peaceful protests."

Jessica Simpson Finds Inner Peace via Proximity to Angelina Jolie!

Spiritual leaders are often known to convey a sense of serenity, a spiritual high, if you will. You hear people say that the Dalai Lama, for example, exudes a remarkable aura. Jessica Simpson finds her inspiration from a different sort of spiritual leader. Angelina Jolie.

As Jess explained: "Just sitting in front of her, I felt this incredible peace."

Kate Hudson Is So Complex, She Likes Skulls!

Kate Hudson thinks she is just *so* esoteric and *so* deep that other people don't get it. She explained that she and then-hub Chris Robinson are incredibly effing complex—and provides a really super-deep example: "We do things that people find hard to understand. For instance, we like skulls. . . . They represent transition, life, and protection." How spiritual! We can't take it!

Lee Ryan's Chicken-Eating Habits Prove He Has Been Reincarnated!

Many celebrities think they may have been reincarnated, but aren't sure. Blues singer Lee Ryan, though, *is* pretty sure . . . because of the way he eats chicken. He claims he *must* have been reincarnated because, "Every time I eat chicken I eat it with my hands . . . like they did in the olden days."

Shirley MacLaine Saw Herself Beheaded!

Shirley MacLaine is one of the foremost "I was reincarnated so many times" celebrities and she's happy to burble on and on and on about it. She has the memories to prove it (man, is she attuned or what?!) and she shares them with everyone, as often as possible. How many of us can recall our past lives? More specifically, how many of us can recall our past deaths—lyrically at that? Shirley can! She described a previous life in which she was beheaded thus: "I watched my head rolling on the floor. It landed face up and a big tear came out of one eye." Brings a tear to our eyes as well. . . . (Interestingly, Shirl has never recalled a life in which she was, say, a large fish. . . .)

Melanie Griffith Travels with Healing Crystal the Size of a Child!

New Ager Melanie Griffith doesn't take any chances with her healing crystals. Bigger is better seems to be her motto . . . so she doesn't just have paltry pissant small crystals to give her the proper karmic energy. She has a big honking four-foot-tall one. It's been said that, loath to leave her four-foot crystal behind when she flies, she'll book an extra seat (in first class) to keep it close at hand.

HOW TO BE MORE SPIRITUALLY ATTUNED: LIFE-ENHANCING TIPS FROM HIGHLY INTELLIGENT CELEBRITIES

How, you are probably asking yourself, can I be more like these incredibly spiritual celebrities? How can I be in touch with my inner self?

As you well might think, celebrities are eager to help you in their own inimitable way.

Tip #1: Be yourself!

"You can expect Bobby to be Bobby. If Bobby ain't Bobby, then Bobby just can't be Bobby."

—BOBBY BROWN

Tip #2: Be proud of what you are!

"The man for me is now the cherry on the pie, but I'm the pie and my pie is good all by itself, even if I don't have a cherry."

—HALLE BERRY

Tip #3: Don't be swayed by other people!

"If I was a giraffe, and someone said I was a snake, I'd think, no, actually I'm a giraffe."

—RICHARD GERE

Tip #4: Be multifaceted (or just plain schizo)!

"I always feel like there's so many spirits in me. I have eight little girls in me. They are wearing miniskirts, they're very cute, always dressed up. I am just a house for them to live. Yeah! One of the girls is a party girl. She's like, 'Let's go party!' I say, 'No, no, no, I'm tired.' She says, 'Let's go party!' The party girl's very stylish, weird. I say, 'That skirt's too short!' She says, 'No, it's not—I have underwear, you don't see nothing.' "

—ACTRESS BAI LING

Five Ghostly Encounters of the Celebrity Kind

It's one of those odd facts: Many celebrities seem to have ghost problems. Is this because ghosts are fans who read the *Star* when they're haunting supermarkets? Or because celebrities are more spiritually evolved so they can see the unseen? Or is it because celebrities are a little . . . out there . . . when it comes to many things, including seeing apparitions?

We are not sure. Well, actually, we have a feeling we might know the answer, but would prefer to take the fifth.

Let us just say that a number of celebrities have had more encounters—and, for that matter, more *up close and personal* encounters—with ghosts than most people.

Celebrity Ghost Encounter #1: Ghost Gives Lucy Liu a Big O

Paranormal researchers have never explained whether or not ghosts have penises. We now know the answer, thanks to Lucy Liu. Yes, ghosts have penises—and they know how to use them. One night, she was sleeping peacefully on her futon on the floor when "some sort of spirit came down from God knows where" and he had sex with her. Transcendental sex, "sheer bliss" as she explained in an interview. "I felt everything. I climaxed. And then he floated away." Just like a typical guy—no chatting, no "was it good for you too?" And he didn't call her again.

Celebrity Ghost Encounter #2: Pervy Peeping Ghost Has Crush on Jennifer Love Hewitt

It's a "life imitates art" (well, "art" for lack of a better term . . .) story. In her TV show *Ghost Whisperers,* Jennifer Love Hewitt communicates with the dead. After researching for her role by meeting with an exorcist, she was plagued by "strange things" happening at her home. (Perhaps the ghosts were critics? We don't know.) She noticed lights mysteriously turning on and off and heard footsteps. But the worst was yet to come. She would shower—and see a ghostly male ogling her nude body. Jennifer immediately applied the knowledge she'd gained from her supernatural research and figured out just what was going on: "The ghost had a crush on me and liked to see me showering."

Celebrity Ghost Encounter #3: Ghost Tries to Get Donald Sutherland to Stop Renovations

Some ghosts just can't give up their day jobs. Donald Sutherland—who starred in the film *An American Haunting* in 2006—was beginning renovations on his 19th-century house when the hauntings began. The culprit? It was a ghost/architect—who apparently wasn't crazy about Sutherland's renovation plans.

Celebrity Ghost Encounter #4: Ghost Pooches Like Robbie Williams

Pop singer Robbie Williams has experience with ghosts of the four-legged kind. Dogs. He sees the spirits of dead Fidos—and quite often. In his impossible-to-misconstrue words: "I've seen ghost dogs. Lots of them." He also has said that he believes that aliens are going to invade the Earth. By the year 2010. Do you think there's any connection here?

Celebrity Ghost Encounter #5: Ghost Doesn't Appear But Gives Off Bad Vibes in Gwyneth Paltrow's House

A source told England's *Daily Mail* that Gwynnie—and husband Chris Martin—hadn't actually *seen* any ghosts, but had felt their presence. Paltrow was worried about "dark energy" in her five-bedroom London town house. In addition, the source said, "her pregnancy is not as peaceful as her last one and she has also been upset by a stalker." Clearly the problem was ghosts, Gwyneth concluded. Logically. So she sought the help of an expert at things spiritual—Madonna. Logically. Madonna helpfully put Gwyneth in touch with a rabbi at the London Kabbalah Centre to set up an exorcism. The heavy-duty ghostbusting ritual would involve 10 men chanting psalms, "a lot more extreme than a Church of England exorcism" in the source's words. Why not move? Well, said a source, Paltrow was "reluctant to move because they spent 1 million pounds renovating the house on top of the 3.5 million pounds they paid for it" (total about $7.75 million). But Paltrow's spokesperson said the report was ridiculous. She "does not feel her home has any bad energy, and, in fact, feels that the house has wonderful energy."

13

THE INTELLECTUAL CELEBRITY

THE INTELLECTUAL CELEBRITY, TO most of us, is an oxymoron—as in "military intelligence." (With a few exceptions. See James Woods, page 18. Did we mention that James Woods has an IQ of 180? Or has he told you already?)

We're here to correct that misconception. The intellectual celebrity is not an oxymoron. It is an impossibility.

The Celebrity "What I Learned in Skool" Test

Let us examine celebrity knowledge by giving them a general information test. Warning to intellectual purists: This is not for those with a heart condition.

Geography

Most celebrities travel a fair amount. They have to jet to a premiere here, a fabulous party there, a yachting vacation here . . . well, you get the drift. So one might assume that geography would be an area they'd have a nodding acquaintance with.

Of course there *are* those celebs who seem less than fascinated by the rest of the world. Like, say, Tyra Banks, back when she was merely a model as opposed to a model/talk show host, who came out with: "I haven't seen the Eiffel Tower, Notre Dame, the Louvre. I haven't seen anything. I don't really care."

But others *do* care! They're citizens of the world! As such, they *know* the world. Or so we assume. . . .

Let's put it to the test. We'll ask celebrities certain rather basic questions about geography and see how well they fare.

1. What is Australia?

"Australia is a beautiful city."

    —TAYLOR HANSON

- Wrong. Australia is a beautiful CONTINENT. (Refresher note: Continents are the big land masses that have countries on them. Some continents are islands. Australia is one of those.) But we can see where Taylor got mixed up since Australia does have cities *on* and *in* it. Maybe this was too much of a trick question . . . ?

2. Is Hawaii a state or a city?

According to singer Tony Bennett, it's a city: "Every city I go to is an opportunity to paint, whether it's Omaha or Hawaii."

- Tony has made a mistake. Hawaii is a STATE. In fact, it is the 50th state. It gets confusing because it is a state made up of several islands (see above)—one of which is named Hawaii. Omaha, however, is indeed a city. Or so we've been told.

3. And what about Louisiana? City or state?

Leo DiCaprio thinks it's a city: "Now, Louisiana is the

second largest consumer of fossil fuels and the city most at risk for sea level rise." (He said this during his Earth Day interview with President Bill Clinton. The quote was cut from the broadcast . . . but printed on salon.com.)

• Wrong-o. Louisiana is a STATE too.

4. What is the capital of New York?

". . . New Jersey?"
—TORI SPELLING

• Nope. We would have even accepted New York City (which, yes, we know is wrong, but at least it's a city). The capital of New York is Albany. Like Louisiana and Hawaii, New Jersey is also a state.

5. If you are in the United States, would you consider Canada—which is a different country from the U.S.— overseas?

Yes, claims Louisiana native Britney Spears, who, when asked the best part of being famous, said: "I get to go to lots of overseas places, like Canada."

• Wrong. You see, Brit, "overseas" has the word "seas" hidden in it. (Yes, it is hard to notice it.) So the implication is that the continent (see above) or country is separated from you by, yes, a sea. Or an ocean. There is no ocean or sea between the United States and Canada. There are a few lakes, but they don't count.

6. Where is England?

"England is in London, right?"
—EMINEM

• Unh-unh, Eminem. We know it's tough to keep track

of, but here goes: London is in England, England is in the United Kingdom, which is in Europe.

7. What is the capital of Uruguay?

"There is no capital of Uruguay, you dummy—it's a country!"

> —LORENZO LAMAS to host Jon Stewart on *The Daily Show*

• Yes and no. Yes, Uruguay is indeed a country. But—an arcane point Lamas failed to grasp—*countries have capitals*! That is why we here in the United States call Washington, D.C., "the capital" (which is not to be confused with "the Capitol building," which is, as you and Lorenzo might have guessed, a building).

8. What would you find in Europe?

Okay, this is a difficult question because it is so broad, but Paris Hilton, bless her brainy head, took a stab at it when she was giving a deposition. Said Ms. Hilton: "I was in Europe the whole summer, and all there is, is like, French."

• Actually, there is, like, more than French in Europe. Correct answers could include the names of European countries (such as Italy, France, etc. etc.), Europeans, and the like. Maybe Paris's name confused her?

Extra credit question (which combines cultural knowledge with geography): Where would one go to attend the Cannes film festival?

Singer Christina Aguilera was asked a variation of this:

INTERVIEWER: "Are you attending the Cannes film festival this year?"

AGUILERA: "I hope so. Where is it being held this year?"

- This is actually correct in the existential sense. To wit, should something happen to Cannes, then the festival might not be there (in Cannes). That said, barring any apocalyptic event happening to Cannes, we can safely assume that the Cannes film festival will, indeed, be held in Cannes. (Which is why it is called the Cannes film festival.) Oh, and Cannes is in France, you know, like, Europe?

CELEBRITIES ASK PRESSING GEOGRAPHICAL QUESTIONS

Let's let the celebrities have a turn here—and have *them* ask some real geographical brainteasers. Don't be upset if you don't know the correct answers.

REPORTER: "Did you realize you have five gold albums in Germany and Austria?"

DAVID HASSELHOFF: "Where's Austria?"

"Do they have palaces in France?"
—SINGER AVRIL LAVIGNE IN AN INTERVIEW, AFTER MENTIONING SHE'D BEEN TO FRANCE AND COULD SPEAK FRENCH

Answers:

1. Austria is in Europe; it is bounded by Slovenia and Italy (S), Switzerland and Liechtenstein (W), Germany and the Czech Republic (N), and Slovakia and Hungary. 2. *Oui.*

History

Next, let's test celebrity knowledge of history.

1. Who is Pericles?

"Pericles? Is he the guy that did the thing with the pota-toes?"

—TARA REID

- No. Pericles didn't do the thing with the potatoes (whatever said thing to which Ms. Reid referred was). In fact, we assume that Pericles didn't do *anything* with potatoes since they weren't available in Greece until after the discovery of the Americas and Pericles was an ancient Greek. Pericles was the guy that did the thing with democracy in Athens. He also ordered the construction of the Parthenon . . . which leads us to our next history question.

2. What is the Parthenon?

Shaquille O'Neal apparently thinks it's a swingin' night-club—as evidenced by his answer when he was asked whether he had visited the Parthenon during his trip to Greece: "I can't really remember the names of the clubs that we went to."

- Shaq is wrong. (We are, however, willing to bet there are a number of souvlaki places around the globe named the Parthenon.) The Parthenon is a large tem-ple of the goddess Athena on the Acropolis in Athens built between 447 and 432 B.C. As far as we know, it doesn't have a bar or a dance floor.

PARIS HILTON'S KNOWLEDGE OF THINGS GREEK

Speaking of Greece—when being deposed for a defamation lawsuit, Paris Hilton was asked about a companion of hers in a nightclub. His first name was Terry, but the lawyer wanted to know his last name. Paris explained: "It is like a weird Greek name. Like Douglas."

(In the spirit of full disclosure, we the authors must inform you that we are of Greek extraction. Oddly, none of our relatives has the last name "Douglas" or even *like* "Douglas.")

3. Who was the president during the Civil War?

"Ummm . . . Winston Churchill? I wasn't around then, so who cares?"

— TOMMY LEE

- Right *and* wrong. Yes, Tommy Lee wasn't around then, but, no, it wasn't Winston Churchill. Winnie was British and was the prime minister during World War II. He made a famous speech that gave the old rock group Blood, Sweat and Tears their name. The president of the United States during the Civil War was American. He was named Abraham Lincoln. Perhaps you've heard of him?

HOW WORLD WAR II COULD HAVE BEEN PREVENTED: HISTORIAN CELEBRITIES WEIGH IN

Celebrities can do almost anything—even stop wars. So let us ask: How would they have stopped World War II, for example?

Take 1: Make Yoko Ono Jewish. Have her have sex with Hitler.

"If I was a Jewish girl in Hitler's day, I would become his girl-friend. After ten days in bed, he would come to my way of thinking."

—YOKO ONO, 1969

Take 2: Blow a blunt. Listen to Bob Marley and the Wailers (for a minimum of three weeks).

"Would it really be possible to start Nazi Germany if you'd just been listening to Bob Marley's *Exodus* back-to-back for the past three weeks and getting stoned? Would the idea of the Holocaust seem so appealing?"

—COLDPLAY'S CHRIS MARTIN IN
THE GUARDIAN

What Happened in World War II Anyway?

Other celebrities, far from having ideas about how to have prevented World War II, have only vague ideas of what happened in the first place. Let's hear from two representatives of this class:

"I didn't know six million Jews were killed. That's a lot of people."

—MELANIE GRIFFITH, STAR OF A
FILM ABOUT JEWS IN GERMANY

REPORTER: "Twiggy, do you know what happened at Hiroshima?"
TWIGGY: "Where's that?"

REPORTER: "In Japan . . . a hundred thousand people died on the spot."

TWIGGY: "Oh, God! When did you say it happened? Where? Hiroshima? But that's ghastly. A hundred thousand dead? It's frightful. Men are mad."

—TWIGGY IN 1968

4. When was the War of 1812?

"I have no clue. 1812? I'm right?"

—TOMMY LEE

- Yes! Tommy Lee is right. The War of 1812 was indeed fought in 1812—something that is obliquely alluded to in its name.

5. Essay question: Discuss Benjamin Franklin.

"I feel really connected to him somehow. He was really quite a guy. Most people just hear about him flying a kite. He did a lot of shit."

—BILLY BOB THORNTON, on the possibility that he is the reincarnation of Benjamin Franklin

- Billy Bob has skillfully demonstrated his knowledge of Ben Franklin. Who among us could argue with his learned statement, "He did a lot of shit"?

Now let's move on while we're on a high note. . . .

Science and Math

1. Tell us about the Pythagorean theorem.

"I'm like the Pythagorean theorem. Not too many people know the answer to my game."

—SHAQUILLE O'NEAL

- Well, see, the problem here is that, unlike Shaq, most people *do* know the "answer" to the Pythagorean theorem. This is the theorem you learn when you're a kid: The sum of the squares of the lengths of the sides of a right triangle is equal to the square of the length of the hypotenuse ($x^2 + y^2 = z^2$). So the answer always is "z^2." But we don't think z^2 is the answer to Shaq's game. (Being tall and big is the correct answer there.)

2. Speaking of triangles, what is an isosceles triangle?

"Somewhere in Bermuda?"

—TOMMY LEE

- Wrong on two counts. First, you don't answer a "what" question with a "where" answer. For example, if someone says, "What the hell is wrong with you?" you don't say, "New York." (Well, maybe you do. One of us lives there and that could be a legit answer some days. But never mind that.) Second, an isosceles triangle is a triangle with two equal sides. The Bermuda Triangle is something different, but we think it might be an isosceles triangle as well.

3. What is pi?

"Pi is pi."

—NICOLLETTE SHERIDAN

- Excellent answer! Pi is most definitely pi. That's why it's called "pi." Perhaps this question was too easy, as easy as, well, pi . . . ? (Sorry. We couldn't help ourselves.) Let's try again.

4. Okay—the revised question: What's the numeric equivalent of pi?

"Is that the 2 = MC squared thing?"

—TOMMY LEE

- No, it isn't. (And, for that matter, that "2 = MC squared thing" shouldn't have a 2 in it; that should be an *e*—*e* as in . . . well, let's say Einstein.) Pi is the ratio of the circumference to the diameter of a circle—and its numeric equivalent is 3.14159265358979323846 . . . (but we would have accepted 3.14). The MC squared "thing" is the theory of relativity.

5. How long does it take for the sun to rotate around the earth?

"My boyfriend gave me [a necklace with a tiny circle on it reminiscent of a planet] . . . because it was our first-year anniversary and it takes like a year for the sun to rotate around the earth."

—KIRSTEN DUNST

- Ha ha! That was a trick question! Actually, the *earth* revolves around the *sun*. (We understand there was a 50/50 chance of getting it wrong . . . if you were Kirsten Dunst, that is.) So do all those other planets in our solar system. (An interesting fact you might not know: It's called "solar" system because of the sun.)

6. Could a dinosaur appear in a movie filmed within the past 20 years? Or even the past century?

This sounds like a trick question, but it isn't. The correct answer is "no." But apparently, Laura Dern believes that dinosaurs *have* been in recent films. As she said, when discussing her film *Jurassic Park*, "You can hardly tell where the computer models finish and the real dinosaurs begin."

- Well, the problem here is that dinosaurs have been *extinct* for many, many years. (Extinct means dead. Dead means they couldn't appear in *Jurassic Park* or any other film. Yes, all those dinosaurs you've seen in films and on TV haven't been real. Shocking, isn't it?)

7. Who invented the polio vaccine?

"Wow. George Bush."
      —TOMMY LEE

- Wow. We are really hoping Tommy Lee was being a cutup. (Jonas Salk.)

Extra credit question (to bring up your score, if needed): How many days are in a week?

We have a hunch you know the answer without even thinking. If so, you are no Jessica Simpson, who—when dazzled by some jeweled pendants at Saks Fifth Avenue in Beverly Hills—said, "I'll take these eight . . . one for every day of the week!"

She was wrong by one. (Which is to say that there are SEVEN days in a week. Not NINE, if that's what you were thinking.)

Religion and Philosophy

Because religion and philosophy are such esoteric topics with a great deal of subjectivity in terms of interpretation and whatnot, we'll dispense with the stricter fact-based questions in the prior sections and, instead, ask celebrities more free-form questions—designed to elicit their deep understanding of these topics.

1. Explain Yom Kippur.

"Who is Yom Kippur? Is that the name of the new Japanese designer?"

> —model turned businesswoman KATHY IRELAND, during a photo shoot when the group began talking about Yom Kippur

• No, Yom Kippur isn't a new Japanese designer, or even an old Japanese designer. Or even a designer. Or a person. It's a major holiday in the Jewish religion—the Day of Atonement. That said, though, many Jewish people do wear nice designer clothing to the temple on Yom Kippur.

2. Explain your religious background.

"Originally my mother was Spanish, then she became a Jehovah's Witness."

> —former Spice Girl GERI HALLIWELL

• Being Spanish is different from being a Jehovah's Witness. Being Spanish is one's *nationality*—the nation (i.e., country) one is from. Being a Jehovah's Witness is one's *religion*—the, well, religion one believes in. We personally believe that one—say Geri's mom—could actually be a Spanish Jehovah's Witness. But we really don't care enough to find out for sure.

3. Essay question: Talk about Kierkegaard.

REPORTER: "Do you read Kierkegaard?"
PAMELA ANDERSON: "Uh, what movies was he in?"

• As far as we know, Kierkegaard (or Søren, as we familiarly call him) wasn't in any movies. Not that he wouldn't have been a heckuva charismatic—if somewhat gloomy—screen presence. Kierkegaard was a philosopher, one of the key figures in "existentialism." We bet he would have done dandy in an Ingmar Bergman film.

Stars on Shakespeare

You may have heard of Shakespeare, William Shakespeare. He's one of those playwrights with whom most people have at least a nodding acquaintance. A long time ago, back when many people actually read books, almost every actor wanted to be in a Shakespearean play. Shakespeare was prestigious, classy, and fun. Back then, almost any actor who was an actor, like Laurence Olivier (Oscar-winning leading man of the '30s) and even William Shatner (*Star Trek*, etc.), got their start in Shakespeare. They *loved* the guy. They pored over his words, memorized favorite passages.

But now . . . well, today our celebrity actors and singers think Shakespeare could use a lot of *improving*.

Celebrity Shakespeare View #1: Shakespeare's too long. They should make an *abridged* version.

This view holds that the immortal Bard is a bit too pro-lix and verbose. In a word, he's boring. Who wants to spend so much time reading all those long words? This view is ex-emplified by Laurence Fishburne (*The Matrix, Mission: Impossible III*), who was recently acting in a modern version of *Othello* in which about two-thirds of the original dialogue had been cut. When a reporter asked Fishburne if he had read the original Shakespeare version of *Othello*, the good thespian tellingly replied:

"Why should I read all those words that I'm not going to get to say?"

Why bother, indeed. The abridged version is *quicker*.

Celebrity Shakespeare View #2: Why bother reading Shakespeare when you get quotes from the Internet? Maybe they should chop the Bard up into bite-size Shakespearelets.

This was evidently the view of Barbra Streisand, who, during a Democratic Party fund-raiser in 2002, delivered a political statement in which she thrillingly "quoted" some of the Bard's immortal lines:

" 'Beware the leader who bangs the drums of war in order to whip the citizenry into a patriotic fervor, for patriotism is indeed a double-edged sword.' "

Babs herself attributed these stirring words to Shake-speare. But she didn't get those lines from reading any of Shakespeare's plays or sonnets, because he never wrote them. Never. They came instead from the Internet, part of an Internet hoax of fake quotes that had been circulating for over a year. But who cares? If faux Shakespeare is good enough for a fund-raiser, it's good enough for us.

Celebrity Shakespeare View #3: Shakespeare's like, too old. And dead. And he has too many *knights* and stuff.

Britney Spears exemplifies this attitude. Once, while taking lessons from one of Hollywood's top acting coaches, she explained that she absolutely didn't want to do Shakespeare:

> "I know who he is, know he's dead, and I don't want any knights-in-armor stuff."

To be fair, Britney wasn't too wild about modern playwrights either; when asked to read from a Harold Pinter play she held up her hand to say no, before scoffing, "Whoever Pinto is, or was." (FYI: Harold Pinter is one of this century's top playwrights.)

(Not to be outdone, her former acting coach had this to say regarding the Shakespeare-disparaging actor-in-training: "Britney is an untalented, self-focused wannabe. I can imagine her ruining a televised drama by suddenly staring straight into the camera and either winking, shaking her boobs, or blowing a bubble of gum. But not all at the same time, that would be asking far too much of her.")

Celebrity Shakespeare View #4: Shakespeare just plain sucks.

Gene Simmons, of the rock group Kiss, takes this enlightened attitude that truly shows the educational attainments and discernment of many of our modern celebrities:

> "I think that Shakespeare is a shit. Absolute shit! He may have been a genius for his time, but I just can't

relate to that stuff. Thee and thous—the guy sounds like a faggot."

Oh, of course. He def can't compete with those incredible KISS lyrics, right?

Deep Concepts from Deep Celebrities

Lest you think that celebrities are shallow morons, we must correct you. Celebrities are not just pretty faces, or talented faces, or whatever-kind-of-faces. They are deep thinkers, people who grapple with esoteric and, indeed, *complex* issues.

We are pretty sure these are the kinds of concepts you too have thought about, but perhaps not in such depth. Ponder them. Think them over. See where they lead *you*.

Cogitating Celebrity: William Shatner
Deep Concept Being Pondered: Suicide

"Take Ernest Hemingway: Here was a guy who swallowed, bit, and orally sucked on the long barrel of a shotgun. What does that tell you? What does it tell you when a guy—in one of the more exotic cases I have heard of—hugs a stove, a hot stove, to death? Horrifying. But what does that tell you?"

What we have learned: What *does* that tell you? We are not sure. Then again, we also are not William Shatner.

Cogitating Celebrity: Keanu Reeves
Deep Concept Being Pondered: Spontaneous combustion

"What would happen if you melted? You know, you never really hear this talked about that much, but spontaneous combustion? It exists! . . . [People] burn from within. . . . Sometimes they'll be in a wooden chair and the chair won't burn, but there'll be nothing left of the person. Except sometimes the teeth. Or the heart. No one speaks about this—but it's for real."

What we have learned: Spontaneous combustion is real. And no one does speak about this. We can't *imagine* why.

Cogitating Celebrity: Julie Delpy
Deep Concept Being Pondered: Imperfection in the world. Such as Hitler. And bitches.

"I know a lot of women who use men, but the world is not perfect. Fifty years ago there was Hitler; now there are bitches everywhere."

What we have learned: Every era has its problems. Back in the '30s and '40s, it was Hitler; now it's bitches. Makes perfect sense.

Cogitating Celebrity: Patricia Arquette
Deep Concept Being Pondered: Government surveillance

"This [the threads in a $20 bill] is so the United States government can scan you. They can tell if you're carrying too much currency. When I showed this to my husband, it really wowed him. When I pulled out this little spy trick, he knew how well he'd done with me."

> —said during an *Us* magazine interview, in which Arquette pulled out a $20 bill, ripped off a corner and pointed out the threads in the bill to the reporter

What we have learned: The government is trickier than we thought. Or Patricia Arquette is a little paranoid. Your call.

FOUR FASCINATING TIDBITS OF ADVICE FROM CELEBRITIES

Many people—possibly rightly—turn to celebrities for advice. Good advice. Very very helpful advice. We think the following might help you with your life.

What You Should Eat: Not Cheese

"Don't eat cheese. There are a million things to eat that aren't cheese."

—COURTNEY LOVE

When to Stay Healthy: While Alive

"I just think the more you can do to maximize your health while you're alive the better."

—GWYNETH PALTROW

How to Determine Past Lives: Your Forehead

"The number of lines in your forehead tells you how many lives you've lived."

—ASHTON KUTCHER

How to Be Lucky (We Think . . . ?): Melons. Or Fortune Cookies. Or Cornflakes.

"Simon gave me advice and said on [the UK show] *The X Factor* he always refers to a fortune cookie and says the moth who finds the melon finds the cornflake always finds the melon and one of you didn't pick the right fortune."

—PAULA ABDUL DURING AN
AMERICAN IDOL SHOW

14

THE CREATIVE CELEBRITY

L ET'S NOW TURN TO one of the most *wonderful* things to happen to the publishing world—celebrity authors generously sharing their talent for writing (in return for advances that are often shockingly low—sometimes less than seven figures!). But the books they offer us are *priceless*. The list of fine celebrity authors goes on and on, from Posh Spice and her insights into a girlhood "gone right" to Pamela Anderson and her insights on breast-growing. And of course, we readers know that with very few exceptions, these books actually are written by the celebrities themselves. Of course.

And we haven't even mentioned poetry.

Yet.

Insights into the Writing Life from Celebrity Authors

Herewith an examination of some of the best of the crop of celebrity authors, along with some of their insights on the "literary life."

Author Posh "You Don't Have to Read Books to Write Books!" Spice (aka Victoria Beckham)

Literary Works: Mrs. Beckham's book *Learning to Fly* was a 528-page autobiography and was the third bestselling non-fiction book in the United Kingdom in 2001. It sold over 500,000 copies.

The author poignantly recounts hearing the theme song from the movie *Fame,* and being particularly struck by the lyrics "I'm going to live forever, I'm going to learn how to fly," which people may recall forms the refrain of the movie's theme song.

Simply put, these flight-as-metaphor-for-success lyrics inspired the young teen (who was sometimes driven to school in her father's Rolls-Royce) to become a success (and later inspired the title of her book). As the book jacket says, "With this amazing book she gives us the chance to fly alongside her on her journey from lonely teenager to international star." An astute reviewer on Amazon.com called it "absoluetely [sic] wonderful." Mrs. Beckham published another work in 2006, *That Extra ½ Inch*—a discourse on fashion, which takes the perhaps controversial position that flats with straight jeans are a no-no.

The Author Speaks:

"I haven't read a book in my life. I haven't got enough time . . . I do love fashion magazines."

Note: Mrs. Beckham now explains that this quote was misunderstood. What she meant to say was that she didn't have time to read a book from "*cover to cover.*"

On fashion book writing: "People love dressing like me so why not profit from it?"

Author Justin "You Don't Even Have to Be Particularly Cognizant of Books to Write 'Em" Timberlake

Literary Works: As yet on indefinite hold due to time considerations. Mr. Timberlake reportedly signed a seven-figure deal with a major publisher for a novel tentatively entitled "Crossover Dribble." The book's story line was secret, but our sources say the book centered on a professional basketball phenomenon named Jason Windriver—who rather unsurprisingly tries to help his team win a championship.

The Author Speaks:

ROLLING STONE INTERVIEWER: "What was the best thing you read all year?"

JUSTIN TIMBERLAKE: "You mean like a book?"

Author Macaulay "All You Have to Do Is String Together Enough Words to Fill a Bunch of Pages and You're an Author!" Culkin

Literary Works: Child actor Mr. Culkin's debut book, entitled *Junior,* is an "audaciously empty mishmash of poems, letters, comics, etc." (*Kirkus Reviews*), and was published by Miramax. Others begged to differ with this reviewer, one calling it a "guilty pleasure," which sounds rather more like masturbation than book-reading—or reviewing. Suffice it to say the book concerns the somewhat random exploits of child-star Monkey-Monkey Boy and another being named Junior. It opens rather cleverly with a five-question quiz that is meant to weed out undesirable readers. Readers here may determine if they consider themselves desirable readers and if they wish to read the book, which, according to a trade reviewer, manages "to lower the already low bar set for celebrity fiction."

Excerpt from the Book:

Dear Dad, Fuck Fuck Fuck Fuck Fuck Fuck Fuck Fuck
Fuck Fuck Fuck Fuck Fuck Fuck Fuck Fuck Fuck Fuck
Fuck Fuck Fuck Fuck Fuck Fuck Fuck Fuck Fuck Fuck
Fuck Fuck Fuck Fuck . . .

. . . etc. etc. I.e., the "fucks" fill a whole page. Readers not too removed from college English courses may deduce that young Culkin's character has rather major father-image problems; could there be shades of something *Oedipal* here? If so, this may be why one positive reviewer liked it, approvingly calling it "complicated."

The Author Speaks: These are further random cullings from the book, which indeed do seem to point to what may charitably be called a complicated mind:

Imaginary, not inflatable, women are okay.

I cried about a steak sandwich one time.

Did you know I have a pet name for my penis [Floyd].

Drink orange juice, because it's good for you.

Sometimes I feel like a 3-foot-tall, poverty-stricken, homosexual, handicapped, 50-year-old Muslim woman with AIDS.

I don't know what the word "urban" means anymore.

Author Snoop "Tell It to the Ladies" Dogg

Literary Works: Mr. Dogg's debut novel, *Love Don't Live Here No More,* is not surprisingly all about a young man growing up in Southern California who aspires to success as a hip-hop star. It sounds maybe a bit autobiographical, but as the book had not yet been published as of this writing, we cannot evaluate it or its plot. So let us allow the publisher's publicist to speak for the novel and its author: "Snoop, by nature of what he does, is a storyteller. Books speak more to a female audience than does his music, so these novels give him an opportunity to show, particularly his female fans, another side." On the female side of things, the author once opined that "Britney would make a better prostitute than Christina. She's thicker"—probably referring to Britney Spears and Christina Aguilera.

The Author Speaks:

On competing titles: "I keep hearing about mutha fucking Harry Potter. Who is this muthafucker?"

On drug use: "So what if I'm smokin' weed onstage and doing what I gotta do? It's not me shooting nobody, stabbing nobody, killing nobody. It's a peaceful gesture and they have to respect that and appreciate that."

Author Naomi "You Don't Even Need to Write Books to Write 'Em" Campbell

Literary Works: Miss Campbell's debut novel, *Swan,* is unusual if only because Campbell's agent actually admitted Naomi didn't exactly write the story of a model's life in her own words. Instead, she *sort of* wrote it. If you're confused, so are we. In the agent's words: "Naomi's very much the author but Caroline [Upcher] is the writer. That's fair. You can't expect Naomi to produce a novel straight off on her own." Maybe you can't. Who are we to quarrel with such a celebrity?

Excerpts from the Book:

Mummy had been right. The beastly press hounds were baying for blood already. I saw them as I slipped across 76th Street at Madison. I refused to let them force me to alter my routine. I crossed Madison as I always did to go and look in Givenchy's window. They always compared me to Audrey Hepburn's Givenchy-clad Holly Golightly in the film of *Breakfast at Tiffany's,* and I suppose I did sort of have something of her dark-haired elfin look.

Sprawled in front of a spin drier, wearing nothing but a pair of white cotton briefs and sneakers, her cropped hair thrown back as she chugalugged a can of Diet Coke, her pierced nose with the chain stretched across her face and running down her lip, Celestia came across on the page as an unmistakably classy piece of ass.

The Author Speaks:

"I just did not have the time to sit down and write a book."

Author Pamela "You Don't Need a Particularly Big Brain to Write Books as Long as You've Got Those Hooters" Anderson

Literary Works: Miss Anderson, if not well known for her brain, is of course quite well known for the other (two) bumps of her anatomy, and her books naturally seem to *focus* on those large and fleshy protuberances. Anderson's output thus far has been two novels, *Star* and a sequel, conveniently named *Star Struck.* Both books are semiautobiographical, and concern a big-breasted star, and (in the second book) a bad-boy rock singer as well (could that be a fictional Tommy Lee?—just speculating), and not too much else. The book flap from the first book essentially sums up the interior content and general literary quality perfectly: "What really happens when A-list meets D-cup?" A pertinent question. Neither book makes for particularly taxing reading, although there are some rather *odd* and vivid scenes, with some interesting vocabulary usages, such as "poisonous node."

Excerpts from the Book:

"Honey," Lucille said, stroking her daughter's hair. "What's wrong?"

"I . . . found . . . a lump," Star managed to choke out.

"A lump?" Lucille asked, confused.

"Right here." Star took her mother's hand and placed it on the poisonous node. "I think it's cancer."

"Oh," Lucille said, drawing back suddenly and laughing as she wrapped her arms around her beloved daughter. "Well, well, well," she said, rocking Star gently. "You're not dying, you're just growing up. Looks like you're finally going to get some boobs. You're becoming a woman, honey. You're blooming!"

And bloom she did. Her breasts came on suddenly and tenaciously, as if trying to make up for lost time. The hard bump turned out to be one of a pair of unruly and self-willed nipples.

"Unruly nipples"?

The Author Speaks:

"I don't think about anything too much. . . . If I think too much, it kind of freaks me out!"

"The book could have been worse—we had to cut stuff out."

Author Katie "Tits and Books Go Together Like . . . Well, Uh, Something" Price (aka Jordan)

Literary Works: The British model and celebrity in her debut novel writes of a young girl who grows up to become a glamorous fashion model, and on the way meets a bad-boy rocker. . . . An astute reader who notices a similarity to the Pamela Anderson literary *oeuvre* is not mistaken. In fact, the author, Miss Price, known to many as the British Pamela Anderson, joins the American author in understanding the value of large heavy dugs. In her words: "Some people may be famous for creating a pencil sharpener. I'm famous for my tits." Along these lines, the author's print appearances prior to publication of her novel are as follows:

- *Playboy's Book of Lingerie* Vol. 58, November 1997, pages 24–25.

- *Playboy's Book of Lingerie* Vol. 59, January 1998, pages 84–89.

- *Playboy's Book of Lingerie* Vol. 60, March 1998, pages 44–47.

- *Playboy's Book of Lingerie* Vol. 61, May 1998, pages 34–35.

- *Playboy's Book of Lingerie* Vol. 65, January 1999, pages 22–23.

- *Playboy's Voluptuous Vixens* Vol. 7, April 2003, cover.

The Author Speaks:

"I read books! I'm more into true crime about murders. My attention span doesn't last very long and when I know it's a true story, I read on because I know it's true."

"I used to like writing stories about horses because I was so into them. Everything was just horses, horses, horses. I actually bought another one at the weekend. I'm nuts! Now I've got him, I have five."

Author Tommy "Who Needs a Brain At All?" Lee

Literary Works: "I want to show you how my memories smell." With this rather interesting choice of words and usages, Tommy Lee introduces us to his "book," appropriately entitled *Tommyland*. It is autobiographical, but it is something more; it helpfully provides the reader with valuable information on how to live life as he does. For example, Mr. Lee discusses in quite vivid detail the mechanics of threesomes and foursomes, leading us (and him) to the inevitable conclusion: Foursomes are far better. You get more horny.

Excerpts from the Book:

There are only so many things you can all do together and there are a few lovely things you can do to both of them at the same time and them to you. But when it comes time for [bleeping], unless there's something out there that I don't know about, you've only got one [sex organ] so there's always someone waiting. The thing to do is have foursomes. Three chicks and just you. If you have three chicks as into one another as they are into you, you can [have sex with] one and watch the other two go at it, which adds to the overall horniness. [I] may increase the number of girls, but [I'll] never be with fewer than three.

The Author Speaks:

"You should mention that I hands-down won the category of Ultimate Pickup Line, for singing the

Oscar Mayer theme song about my penis over the phone to Pamela."

(Note for the curious: The puckishly *clever* song began with "My baloney has a first name, it's p-e-n-i-s . . .")

OTHER CELEBRITY AUTHORS ON BOOKS

"I'm starting to read to my son. But I couldn't believe how vapid and vacant and empty all the stories were. There's, like, no lessons. . . . There's, like, no books about anything."
—MADONNA IN AN INTERVIEW ABOUT THE CHILDREN'S BOOK SHE HAD WRITTEN

AUTOBIOGRAPHY—OR NADABIOGRAPHY?

What is an autobiography? Usually, it's a story of the life of the person who wrote it. Unless you're a celebrity. Then it's about . . . nothing—which is not to cast aspersions on the interior of the average mind of the celebrity. Well, not necessarily. . . .

"I want an autobiography without revealing any personal information whatsoever."
—DIANA ROSS TO HER EDITOR

"To say this book is about me (which is the *main* reason I was uncomfortable—me, me, me, me, me . . . frightening!) is ridiculous. This book is not about me."
—KATE MOSS ON HER BOOK, *KATE: THE KATE MOSS BOOK*

Celebrity Poetry

Ah, poetry!

The Songs of the Muses! We don't read or hear enough poetry nowadays. Poetry is an art that is dying. But fortunately, we now have our celebrity poets, who are keeping this wonderful form of expression alive and *vibrant.*

Mariah Carey, the Children's Poet

Mariah Carey, better known as a singer of sorts, announced plans to publish a poetry book for children. Included in her proposal was this heart-warming piece every little one should just *love,* particularly because it all *rhymes!* Plus, it's not at all hard to follow. We're quite certain that editors just snapped this proposal up. Students of the craft of poetry who are lucky enough to read the entire poem will note that the poem follows a classic AABB rhyme scheme. And note the clever nomenclature of the unicorn. The reader approaches the second line with some trepidation, wondering: *What will the poet name the unicorn?* And then the answer comes . . . Boo, of course! Naturally, as it rhymes with "true." Why didn't we think of that? Ah, but we cannot all be poets.

AN EXCERPT FROM "THE UNICORN"

I love my unicorn, he knows I am true,
My troubles go poof, my unicorn named Boo

Britney Spears, the Poet of Love

Britney Spears follows Mariah Carey in the discovery of the AABB style of rhyme, but she offers a more advanced poetic style, probably because her poem is aimed at a more mature audience. Readers should take note of her clever rhymes. We can see that while Dante had his Beatrice, Britney had her K-Fed (at least, *then* she did), and it is difficult to say who was the more *inspired*.

AN EXCERPT FROM "HONEYMOON POEM"

Silence is golden, no running cars.
Private dinners, romantic fires

Charlie Sheen, Beat Existentialist

Sheen follows a more complicated pattern of AAAAABBBBB, and pursues a more complicated theme—i.e., time flies. One question: In the excerpt below, why "peace" and not "piece"? Is this the poet's playful way of telling us that the two are somehow synonymous? Or does he have a spelling problem? Or is it simply a typo? Also, why the imposition of sailing imagery, which comes out of nowhere?

I'm headin' to sea as I raise the mast.
Oh, teacher, teacher, I'm a peace of your past.

Kevin Federline: Hip-Hop's Rich White (Ex-)Husband

The Former Mr. Spears takes life on the angry streets of Malibu and translates it into the edgy vernacular of hip-hop. His musical abilities are of course the stuff of legend, or at least discussion, and his lyrics are similarly regarded. The following is a selection from the Former Mr. Spears's earlier works; the song "Y'All Ain't Ready" proved startlingly true in its message since no record company backed it. Instead, it was released on the Internet for all to ponder, for there is, after all, an essential truth in its message, at least in regard to the money.

Go ahead and say whatcha wanna
I'm gonna sell about two mil, fool, then I'm a goner . . .

CELEBRITY GOSSIP BLOGS WE LOVE
(and you might, too . . .)

TheSuperficial.com ("A brutally honest look at society and its obsession with the superficial")

Jossip.com ("Celebrity + Media + Manhattan")

Gawker.com ("Manhattan media news and gossip")

IDontLikeYouInThatWay.com ("The sexiest site on the Internet")

PinkisthenewBlog.com ("Everybody's Business Is My Business™")

TMZ.com ("A 24/7 on-demand news network on the Web")

Eonline.com ("The latest daily news and celebrity inside information in a fun, irreverent tone")

PopSugar.com ("Insanely addictive")

Defamer.com ("The L.A. gossip rag")

PerezHilton.com ("Celebrity Juice, Not from Concentrate")

ACKNOWLEDGMENTS

Many thanks to our wonderful editor, Bruce Tracy; our incredible production editor, Beth Pearson; and our fabulous agent, Celeste Fine.

ABOUT THE AUTHORS

KATHRYN PETRAS and ROSS PETRAS are siblings, and the authors of the national bestselling "Stupidest" series as well as other humor books. Their titles include *Unusually Stupid Americans*, *The 776 Stupidest Things Ever Said*, *Stupid Sex*, and *Very Bad Poetry*. Their work has received the attention of such personalities as David Brinkley and Howard Stern, publications including *The New York Times*, *Playboy*, *Cosmopolitan*, *The Washington Post*, and the London *Times*, and television shows including *Good Morning America*. They are also the creators of the number one bestselling *365 Stupidest Things Ever Said Page-A-Day Calendar* (now in its thirteenth year).